*Gone so soon,
with all the dedicated work she had done...
we will continue with the work she has left behind.
showing people "God's Love and Care"
Emmanuel Mwesigye*

CONTENTS

Foreword ... xi

1. Put a Clearance Around Your Garden ... 1
2. How We Get Cream - Cow Ghee ... 7
3. Lord to Give Us the Ability to Keep Our First Love ... 13
4. No Service For Christ Goes Unnoticed by Him ... 19
5. To Make the Most of Today Keep Eternity in Mind ... 25
6. The Best Role Models - Model Christ ... 27
7. Managing Problems Positively ... 31
8. Duo Ngikuhaire, I Have Given You Double ... 35
9. The Universe is Full of the Presence of God ... 39
10. Sister Judi Zak ... 41
11. How do I Keep From Feeling So Small ... 47
12. The Presence of God ... 53
13. Seek the Reviver - Not the Revival ... 59
14. Where Did Evil Come From? ... 63
15. I am Christ Who Called You ... 67
16. With God is Synergy ... 71
17. You Are the Forerunner ... 75
18. Closeness, Nearness, Intimacy ... 79
19. You can Never see the Sunrise by Looking to the West ... 83
20. Path of Least Resistance Makes Men and Rivers Crooked ... 91
21. The Most Exciting Journey Will Never Take Place Unless You Take the First Step ... 95
22. Six Barren Women ... 101
23. Envy provides the mud and failure thrown at success ... 107
24. Can an extension function without being plugged in? ... 111

25. Grab our Brethren Back	117
26. God Makes a Podium for His People	121
27. Do You Not Fear the Lord?	125
28. Look for the Ancient Paths	135
29. Unpurchasable	139
30. You are my Bride	143
31. Friendship and Relations	145
32. Self involvement, another spiritual trap	147
33. If I Ask You to Do Something Extraordinary Will You Do It?	151
34. Why Do I Look Like A Soldier Right Now?	155
35. The Journey Has Started	159
Acknowledgments	163
About the Author	165

WORD OF THE LORD FOR GERTRUDE KABATALEMWA

I believe I heard the Lord say
You are a General - in His army
You are a woman of valor
You are a woman of great faith
Those who have preceded you and those that will follow

There is not one with a greater faith as you
You are an Apostle - there will be more churches established
Training up those in your care now to begin other church groups
As His message of salvation and love continues to be spread throughout the nation

I believe I heard the Lord say
Your job is not done
You have accomplished much but
There is much more to be accomplished
He has given you a great vision
And those to stand with you in bringing forth this vision
You cannot do this alone

I believe I heard Him say
Begin to seek Him
There are those who are now working in various projects
But He will begin to show you - one by one-
Those whom He will raise up to walk beside you
To further along and to fulfill the vision
Walking with you in unity, harmony and one accord
To accomplish the same vision He has given you
You to delegate responsibility for various projects to those He shows you
So that you can be freed up to begin new endeavors
And to further along others

Multiplication - multiplication of help - more people to be set in place to help you
To take on more of the work that needs to be done
Delegation - your delegating more work to others to free up yourself

He will continue to provide for you
Finances help in all you need
The vision is expanding
More will be started
More will be accomplished

And I believe I hear the Lord say
The angels of the Lord encamp around you
And continue to be at your side
To protect you and provide for the needs
Rest in peace knowing that even greater things are in store
Greater things will be accomplished

And I believe I hear the Lord say

You have been found faithful
He loves you very much

And the Lord says to you
"Well done My good and faithful servant!"

Sunday Mar 28, 2010 Approximately 5:20 PM

FOREWORD

We may not agree with what Ms. Gertrude Kabatalemwa has written. It may not be politically correct for our generation. But, let us get passed our judgements, and hear the heart of this African woman.

If so, we will find ourselves understanding a depth of spirituality that will most likely be lost to the next generations.

AFRICA HAS SOMETHING TO SAY TO US.

May we listen intently with raw ears to hear a direction that could keep our future from becoming sterile.

Teresa Skinner
All Nations International

CHAPTER ONE
PUT A CLEARANCE AROUND YOUR GARDEN

FOR TWO DAYS the Holy Spirit put on my heart the Story of Eli and his two sons Hophni and Phinehas, Samuel 2:3-5.

Prayer, Lord, raise me for Yourself a faithful maid servant, who shall do according to what is in Your heart and in Your mind. Build me a Sure House, and that I shall go in and out before you anointed Forever. *4th June 2011*

A FRIEND CAME WHILE MY HEART WAS STILL HEAVY WITH this message. When I shared with her she was in agreement with me that the Lord gave it to her sometime back to share it at Kasozi Prayer Mountain with the Pastors.

People of God who are in leadership, e.g. fathers, mothers, guardians, pastors, and elders, are not helping to raise their children, young Christians who are coming to know the Lord. They fear to rebuke them or to council them in pure love for the Lord. Christians poison their own children for fear that they will discontinue to help them or not bring a big offering in the offering basket and tithe, even when they know that they are in fornication, doing wrong business for example; selling liquor, gambling business, cheating, prostitution etc. Fathers, mothers and pastors just keep quiet for fear of not offending them that they stop coming to church.

This was the sin of the high priest Eli, when he was told that his sons were not honouring God's mens sacrifices which they brought to offer before the Lord, they were fornicating with the temple maids in front of God's presence. God sent a man who told Eli all what was going to happen to him and his sons, but Eli could not call his sons and give them a warning, or give them a suspension, and they continued annoying God. Again God called Samuel, a young boy who used to sleep in the temple of the Lord, and told him the same message to tell Eli, because Eli was so old he had not corrected his sons to fear the Lord when they were still young; the saying: You straighten the stick when it is still young when it grows old it becomes hard."

Due to fear of correcting his sons the following disasters befell Eli's home: 1) his sons Hophni and Phinehas died on the same day, 2) the Ark of the Lord was captured by the Philistines, 3) Eli himself died, 4) forty-three thousand (43,000) men of Israel died as children were left orphans and wives were left widows, 5) the wife of Phinehas died giving birth, and Ichabod, the glory of the Lord left Israel cause the Ark was captured by the heathen. The Ark stayed out of the temple for over twenty years, and the Israelites lamented after the Lord.

All this will happen to you if you refuse to correct your children, your flock they will marry and be married to ungodly spouses, they will die of AIDS, etc. The presence of the Lord will depart from your house. You will die yourself in agony. People of God will scatter and some will die.

The Glory of the Lord will depart. *8th June 2011*

PUT A CLEARANCE AROUND YOUR GARDEN.

Message, I was returning from the village after 2 weeks with the Youth Team from Louisiana. I was so fatigued I felt sick and Emma came to pick me. On the way I got this message: Put a Clearance Around Your Garden. It is necessary when you prepare your garden put a clearance around your garden to separate the it from over grown grass. leeches and weeds from close by bushes, creeping vines, scourge grass, shadows from close nearby bushes, rats, rabbits, and snakes from crossing over.

When you do not put a clearance around your garden, it will attract enemies to encroach your garden. It's not easy to keep and tend a garden which is mixed up with the bushes because everything mentioned above creeps in at will and you have no control over it but when the clearance is there it deters them before they go far.

So, a Christian's life is like the protected garden with a clear boundary to keep away the creeping vines, overgrown, scourge grass and weed bushes which tries to cross over and entangle the plants. The clearance scares the rats, rabbits and snakes because of the light. The clearance there will be no shadow over your garden which obscures your plants from light.

As a Christian you should put a clearance boundary in your Spiritual walk. Keep your garden separated from close by bushes, because they habour the enemy of your beautiful garden, they are always looking for ways and means of crossing. Remember once your garden was part of that bush, but since you separated yourself, the creepy, the weed, the leaches were not happy to leave them there and become a beautiful, fruitful garden which feeds the hungry; everybody in this world gets hungry, from a king to a pauper. *15th June 2011*

REPENT, FORGIVE THEM AND PRAY FOR THEM

Message, Repent, Forgive Them and Pray for Them for God's Grace. I got this message: All those who wronged you will come back and ask for forgiveness like in Job. People have not got heaven for you. It is ME who have heaven for you. Your enemies will be put in a corner where they shall not come out until they come before you for help. All what they accused of you, they will come and tell to you and repent before the open, even that what was said in secret they will tell you in tears and ask you for your forgiveness. They will say we were wrong and you were right. I will vindicate for you. *22nd June 2011*

Early in the morning again I was so disturbed and asked myself the following questions:

Why do people think I am wrong? Why am I isolated? Why are all my relatives have kept aloof? Why do people think I am difficult? Is it me who is wrong or they are wrong?

After asking myself all this for almost two days, I decided not to go to work today but remain in the presence of God, the Holy Spirit lead me to start praying that the Holy Spirit would get me the answers to these questions.

Immediately I got a solution: To Repent, Forgive and Pray for my enemies. First to repent of judging others, condemning and pointing fingers to others, Second to forgive all those who have wronged me by talking, thinking, imagining, and desiring evil against me. Third to pray for all those who wronged me and ask for the Lord's grace to have mercy upon them.

When we repent, forgive and pray for our enemies God opens spiritually, physically and materially the doors and windows which were closed by the unforgiveness sin. He repairs the bridges which were broken, closes doors and windows which were open. He re-opens wells which were blocked. This is a great key for the Kingdom of God, the Word says if you do not forgive you will also not be forgiven, Matthew 6. *23rd June 2011*

Guests with Kabatalemwa at farm after donation of tractor

CHAPTER TWO
HOW WE GET CREAM - COW GHEE

DREAM, we were traveling with Emma, in a corner around the bush I saw a rare pink bird which I have never seen anywhere, not even in the World Bird's Book. I kept watching it as it had rare tunes like a human and gestures. When it opened its plumage like a peacock nothing could be compared to a peacock. I ran and caught it and was very delighted to have it in my arms. We reached home, it seemed I had been away for sometime. First, I prayed on its head: You will not run away, you will not die, you will not be stolen, if Jesus returns soon or later you will still be with me.

I was holding it all the time. I got my beautiful cup and a container with golden rims and started washing them, and telling the beautiful bird that this is going to be your cup and a container where you will be drinking and eating from, and the bird was acknowledging like a human being that.

When I finished rinsing the cup and the container, I put water in the cup for it to drink.

Immediately a puppy which I had left in the house was very hungry, the bird came out of my hands and ran into the corner of the house and all over a sudden came to drink, and the puppy jumped and started chasing it, at first I thought they were going to be friends, but to my surprise it started chewing its head. I jumped and opened its mouth and got out the bird's head and feared it was already hurt. I kicked the puppy very hard sending it reeling out of the house and picked the bird into my hands again, as I was holding it in my arms it started wiggling its head in my arms and life started getting back into its head. I woke up and prayed, that if it was the enemy's disguise to come so close to me I rebuked it, and if the dream is from the Lord to tell me my future blessing how the enemy was trying to hurt it, I declare victory over it. *25th June 2011*

AFTER EARLY MORNING PRAYERS I HEARD THE WORD: National Event, I saw 95%, as I saw Uganda's flag kind of covering a box, the crested crane not seen. *27th June 2011*

EARLY IN THE MORNING IN A DREAM I SAW PRESIDENT Museveni in a far country standing with many other presidents in a line, each one having a turn to hit the ball as it is done in volleyball. When the turn of Museveni came the ball was in his view, I thought he was going to hit it but he did not, it fell at his feet, he closed his hands as in prayer and started shaking his head as one in deep spirit. At that time, I read in the News paper of 30th June 2011, New Vision, that he was attending AU Conference in Malabo in Equatorial Guinea, in Central Africa.

On this same day early in the morning when I was praying, I got a Message:

How We Get Cream - Cow Ghee:

- Pure Milk has to be kept for three to four days in order to get sour/stale
- At times crude salt was dropped in the milk to quicken staleness
- Then it is put in a calabash, a big gourd (Ekisabu)
- Churning was done at dawn by young strong virgin maidens of the home
- Hard shaking with up and down strokes
- After hard shaking the milk would get to first stage of frost, then the frost would spread, after spreading it would form small lumps, turn into big lumps and then with a gentle movement the milk would separate with the cream and the lumps would become one big cream.
- Separation, The waste milk is removed. from the calabash (Kisabu) and given to dogs, cats and commoners or poured at the backyard (Mukibanga).
- Only cream is left there, at times the cream was left there for 2-3 churns.
- When the cream is removed from the vessel it is washed in salty water to remove the impurities. This is done by squeezing, patting, rinsing and draining out all the stale milk.
- Lastly the churning vessel, is cleaned when it delays to process cream because of contamination, in the local language it is called 'to make it vomit' special herbs are used, after that it is smoked and scented to give good smell.

Uses of Cream (Ghee): includes a) healing properties - heals, embalms, it soothes hash smelly medicine, b) makes good rich source - Kitaama (eshabwe), c) cream softens hardness, softens tightened hard lids and covers, d) cream adds taste, gives different taste to food, e) it repels insects when poured on their path, f) is good for the skin treated g) essential scented cream is expensive cream for the bride, and h) is used in palaces for the king's special dishes.

Process of Cream, to get cream, there are processes it has to go through, some creams take short time others long time to yield. This depends on the type of cow, because some cows give light easy milk which yields fast. Other cows give hard milk which takes a long time to yield, this means one has to churn hard and take long to yield. Both processes depend on the type of cow's milk, easy yielding or hard, therefore the one who is churning has to be aware of the pressure and strokes to apply. During the process the young maidens sing praise songs naming each favourite cow and the type of milk they yield. These songs brought joy, vigor and rhythm of movement. This also would bring quick yield of cream, e.g. praise and worship.

Separation, For whom he did foreknow, he also did predestinate to be conformed to the image of his Son, that he might be the firstborn among many brethren. Romans 8:29

All things work together and are fitting into a plan for good and for those who love God and are called according to His design and purpose. Romans 8:28

You were created clean and pure as pure as milk. After some time the enemy started to pollute you slowly, until you became stale, but the Lord in His mercy and grace picked you up and placed you in a vessel, in the hands of His servants and maid servants to shake out of you the old nature and turn you into pure cream after getting out of you all the impurities, so that you reach the unreachable, He makes you sits in high places with kings and rulers of the earth.

You cannot get cream unless it is churned and has gone through processes. When the Lord got you, you were living in

this stale, wicked, evil world and some of you or us who had's over stayed he had to induce them to stale fast.
Each one of us know where He got us, e.g. witchcraft, prostitution, drunkenness, thief, etc. You know how long you lived in the state of staleness in the world for 20, 30, or 40 years before you came to Christ. When you came out of the stale world you were put in a churning vessel, e.g. church, fellowship or home sell.

PROCESS, THE PROCESS YOU WENT OR GOING THROUGH, IS IT HARD OR EASY FOR YOU TO YIELD?

Your process to turn into cream depends on your ability to do what the Word is saying, obedience, faith and trust in the Lord. At times your process is delayed due to state of a churning vessel (church) itself; if the vessel is contaminated, it needs to be cleaned (to make it vomit), let the church repent, fast and pray, then the Lord will smoke and put good scent in it, so that people will smell it from very far and say we want to go to such and such a church. If you are hard and still hanging on the old nature, you will go through long process and hard strokes will be applied to bring you to the place where God wants you.

Songs of praise, worship, repentance and songs telling situations and history what you went or are going through help to focus and come to the place where the Lord wants you to be.

Stages of process, After going through all the shaking and pounding with the Word of God aA new Christian at times filled with the Holy Spirit for the first time you see her or him running in circles, falling on the ground, at times foaming, yelling or shaking. Some churches say that the demons are leaving.

After all that craziness which at times takes weeks or months depending on how involved or possessed you were in the evil, wicked, and stale world, when all that is gone he of she starts coming to self and settles down.

Then you join groups like the ladies, men, youth, or choir at this stage the world will be drained out of your life and you cannot lie, drink, smoke, run after the other sex person, steal, etc.

Last but not least you find yourself a big Evangelist, Pastor, Ladies Group Leader, etc. and you are a cream with many uses for Jesus as given above. *28th June 2011*

CHAPTER THREE
LORD TO GIVE US THE ABILITY TO KEEP OUR FIRST LOVE

AS IT WAS on 1st October 2010 in the message of Obedience and Disobedience, you can be told to eat or not to eat and in both you can disobey or obey. Again, a meal of meat I was told not eat but I ate was Disobedience. On 1st October 2010 a meal from the same place with meat as I was fasting on meat and was told to eat the meat and I ate was Obedience. Amazing. I started a long fast of all delicacies, e.g. meat, sugar, milk and others until 23rd August 2011 when I was traveling to US for the funeral of Sis Judi, that is when I broke the fast in the plane. *1st July 2011*

I WOKE UP IN A PRAISING MOOD AND DECIDED TO START revising the 45days of Preparation the Lord gave me from 2nd October to 16th November 2010.

Message, David makes Solomon king, 1 Chronicles 29:14,

Prayer of Solomon, 2 Chronicles 1:7-12,

In love He predestined us according to the purpose of His Will, Ephesians 1:3-14. *2nd July 2011*

PRAYER, LORD WHEN YOU SEND ME WHERE YOU NEED TO send me let me be Myself not to copy what others are doing, Be Natural, keep myself as you created me, not to change my outlook spiritually or physically I know you are pleased the way I conduct myself and I look. Be Normal, let me not be superficial or super spiritual, let me see things both in spirit and in natural. Be Relaxed, let me learn to rest in you always and not overwork the body which accommodates the Spirit, the Spirit cannot work effectively when the body is tired.

Prayer, Lord be gracious to me, I have waited expectantly for you. Be the arm of your maid servant, her defense and strength every morning, my salvation in the time of trouble, Isaiah 33:2. Amen.

But who is able to build Him (God) a house, since heaven, even the highest heaven, cannot contain Him? God is so high, so big that even the highest heaven cannot contain Him, we should give Him due respect and fear Him. Then Hiram king of Tyre recognized king Solomon: Because the Lord loves His people. He has made you king over them also he said Blessed be the Lord, the God of Israel who made heaven and earth, who has given to David the king a wise son endued with prudence and understanding who should build a house for the Lord, 2 Chronicles 2:6,11.

When you obey, love, honour, and give Him due respect and walk before Him even the heathen who worship idols will recognize your God and call Him Lord. He raised us up together with Him and made us sit down together giving us joint seating with Him in the heavenly sphere by virtue of being in Christ Jesus the Messiah the Anointed one. Ephesians 2:6. *3rd July 2011*

In this scripture I learnt how people get used to and later results in familiarity both to God and man and physical things. I have come to understand from the whole chapter 3, where king Solomon built the House of the Lord for the Lord of Lords and King of kings of which God Himself gave the Blue Prints. He overlaid most of the inside and the vessels with pure gold. I guess when it was finished everybody was so proud to have such land mark structure standing in Jerusalem on Mount Moriah, 2 Chronicles 3.

As time went by the very people who used to admire and boast of the Beautiful Temple started looking at it like any other building around, instead of going to worship in there they started by passing it and going to worship Baal, and the Lord caused the heathen to come and destroy it as He had promised.

As it was with the Temple of Solomon, also God Himself, people when freshly have come to know Him think they can do anything, but as time goes by they grow cold and start doing their own things. There is a lady minister at a church who annoys me so much, whenever she is ministering, there is an annoying comment she makes "Myabula Nyanya" after mentioning the name of the Lord. That is familiarizing.

This applies to everyday walk, husbands get used to their wives they used to worship and later wives get used to their husbands they used to worship and later people get used to their newly built house and later see no longer of their beauty, when people buy their new vehicles, they worship them and later they no value.

WE SHOULD ASK THE LORD TO GIVES US THE ABILITY TO KEEP OUR FIRST LOVE.

In Ephesians 3 apostle Paul states To me the very least of all the Saints I was given grace. This is because Paul was not among the 12 apostles of Jesus Christ not even a Disciple. But he was called to preach the gospel to the gentiles the Unfathomable, unheard of Riches of Christ and to bring to light what is the Administration of the Mysteries which were hidden in God for ages who created all things, so that the unfolding wisdom might be made known through His people, the Church,, to the rulers and authorities in the heavenly places.

What are the Unfathomable Riches and Mysteries which were hidden? They are Interpretation of God's Word, the revelation of who God our Father is, revelation of who Christ is, faith in Jesus Christ, dreams and interpretation of dreams, miracles and wonders. *4th July 2011*

THE ARK OF THE LORD IS BROUGHT IN THE TEMPLE AND THE GLORY OF THE LORD FILLS THE TEMPLE.

When all the priests came out of the sanctuary of Holy Place they had all sanctified themselves regardless of their divisions. All singers standing on the east of the altar and 120 priests all blowing trumpets, with one voice in unison, one voice, to Praise and Glorify the Lord, the house of the Lord was filled with the Cloud.

Even this time if people of God sanctify themselves and come together the glory of the Lord will come down and fill the house, 2 Chronicles 5:11-14.

Be imitators of Christ who gave himself up for us an offering and sacrifice to God as a fragrant aroma. Take no part have no fellowship and do no business with the unGodly, but instead let your lives be so in contrast as to expose and disprove and convict them. for it is shame to speak or mention the things that such people practice in secret e.g. former mayor of Kampala (Seya) having witchcraft kettle where he kept Museveni, they said that what even he said he would consent. When everything is exposed to the light it is made visible and clear. The Lord says; Awake O sleeper and raise from the dead and Christ shall shine upon upon you and give you light. Isa. 26:19, 60:1-2.

Look carefully then how you walk! Live Purposefully and Worthily and Accurately, not as the unwise and witless but as Wise, Sensible, Intelligent people making the very most of the time buying up each of the time opportunity by using every minute profitably because the days are evil. Therefore, do not be vague, thoughtless and foolish, but understanding clarity and firmly grasping what the will of God is for you. Do not get drunk with wine for that is debauchery with the Holy Spirit, Prov. 23:20. Speak out to one another, your self in psalms hymns and spiritual songs making melody in your heart to the Lord and At all times give thanks to the Lord Jesus Christ to God the Father, Ephesians 5:1-20. *5th July 2011*

THEN THE LORD APPEARED TO SOLOMON AT NIGHT AND SAID to him; I have heard your prayer ... If I shut up the heavens so that there is no rain, or if I command the locust to devour the land, or if I send pestilence among my people and my people who are called by my name humble themselves and pray and seek my face and turn from their wicked ways, then I will hear from heaven, will forgive their sin and will heal their land. 2 Chronicles 7:12-14.

Advice to children, parents, and slaves take the armor of God so that you will be able to resist the wiles of the enemy. Ephesians 6:13. The work of the Lord for us has been done. Jesus has paid the supreme sacrifice for God has only begun and nothing we do can help pay the Price. Christ's Work on the Cross equips us to do good work for Him. *7th July 2011*

CHAPTER FOUR
NO SERVICE FOR CHRIST GOES UNNOTICED BY HIM

JONI EARECKSON TADA said to see Jesus will be heaven's greatest Joy, for me, this will be the best part of heaven. Eye has not seen, nor ear heard ... the things which God has prepared for those who love Him, 1 Corinthians 2:9. She said "What a blessing to offer 'a praise that is pure' with no wandering thoughts, no self-centered requests, no inability to soar above my earth-bound language!" *8th July 2011*

MESSAGE FROM OUR DAILY BREAD,
Prayer, Set me afire Lord, stir me I pray. While the world is perishing I go your way purposeful and passionate day after day.

"Tough Times Never Last, But Tough People Do"

ROBERT SCHULLER

Set me afire, Lord, stir me up I pray. Amen,

"Great people are just ordinary people with an extraordinary amount of determination. They simply don't know how to quit."

PASTOR RICK WARREN

Have faith with hanging over power! The ingredient of this is mountain-moving faith, miracle-generating faith, earth shaking faith, problem-solving faith and situation-changing faith are the ingredients of all this is holding on power.

"Your life will become a light for someone else's pathway."

When the roads, community, and situations are rough, the tough ones rise to the occasion, they win. They survive. They come out on top!

"When the going gets tough, the tough get going."

KNUTE ROCKNE

The story of a potatoes farmer who never sorted his potatoes but would put all the potatoes in a wagon and drive the rough road and the potatoes would sort themselves, the small at the bottom, the medium next and the big ones on the top. The law of life is big potatoes rise to the top on rough roads, and tough people rise to the top in rough times.

"Possibility Thinking Works."

MARIA VON TRAPP IN SOUND OF MUSIC

15th July 2011

BE STEADFAST, IMMOVABLE ALWAYS ABOUNDING STEADFAST in the works of the Lord knowing your labour is not in vain in the Lord. 1 Corinthians 15:58.

No service for Christ goes unnoticed by Him. *16th July 2011*

AFTER THE EARTHQUAKE IN SAN FRANCISCO, A YOUNG BOY was seen rocking and swinging on school ground, when the principal asked him if he was ok, and the boy nodded yes and said, I am moving like the earth, so if there is another earthquake, I will not feel it. He wanted to prepare himself for another shaking of the ground. To survive the storms of life, be anchored on the Rock of Ages. *17th July 2011*

PROPHESY CANNOT BE PROVED AS A FACT UNTIL IT COMES TO PASS

Message, "Beware of false prophets ... in sheep's clothing, but inwardly they are ravenous wolves. Matt. 7:15. God's word gives wisdom to discern what is false.

On this day when I returned home, I found the notorious palm tree beside my bedroom chopped down into 11 pieces, I praised the Lord, because the Word of God I received on 8 July 2010 had come to pass. Glory be to God. In the Word of God on my iPad said "The Prophesy cannot be proved as a fact until it comes to pass."

Out of this tree came out all kinds of noise whenever I started to pray, in dreams and trance I would see demonic power coming out to attack me and strange birds used to make it their resting place. Since the Lord told me that the day it will fall that is when I will leave this place. I kept a watch on it, and wondered which side it would fall as it was so tall close to the house and electric wires, and I prayed; Lord, when it falls let it not fall on my bedroom or across the electric wires. But look the greatness of our Lord it did not fall but it was cut.

As soon as when I entered the house in September 2006 and saw in the spirit that this tree was harboring evil spirits, I cursed it and used to pray facing it and addressing the evil spirits which used to manifest in terrible noises of tins, cracking, booms, there would be wind swaying when there was no wind anywhere else. I commanded that one day you tree shall wither from the stem to the top and I kept watching it, and within my notice one twig after twig started withering until the Lord gave me the prophesy and finally cut it down. Praise the Lord! When it was cut, I waited 8 months until 1st March 2012 we left the house. *18th July 2011*

Message, king Uzziah became a giant through the Lord's blessing, Zechariah instructed him, God prospered him, and later his heart was lifted up to his destruction. He went to perform the duties which were not his as he went to offer incense in the temple which was the duty of priests and Uzziah ended a leper cut off from the house of the Lord, 2 Chronicles 26:3-21.

When we become strong, we must take heed or we too will stumble. I have never met a man who has given me trouble as myself and my flesh. Daily Bread: Small Step, Giant Step. *9th July 2011*

This is when Neil Armstrong became the first human to set foot on the moon and he said "That's one small step for man; and one giant leap for mankind." Each small step in faith is a Giant step of growth. *20th July 2011*

Children Praying

Secondary student class

CHAPTER FIVE
TO MAKE THE MOST OF TODAY KEEP ETERNITY IN MIND

ETERNITY IN OUR HEARTS, On my visit to an Aquarium in Chicago March 2006 and the Long Beach Pacific Aquarium in February 2011, seeing the dazzling clarity the beauty the Lord created under water I was left breathless, but the most amazing wonder is "God had put eternity in my heart."

Ecclesiastes 3:11, such an elegant phrase applies, tells, and calls to attention much in human experience. Surely it hints at a religious instinct. Our hearts receive eternity in ways other than the religious. It calls for deeper relationship, cultivation, and focusing.

Ecclesiastes presents both sides of life here on this planet: the promise of pleasure so alluring, enticing the we may devote our lives to that pursuit or chasing haunting realizations that these pleasures ultimately do not satisfy. To chase these tantalizing worldly pleasures is too big, humongous for mankind. Unless we acknowledge our limits and subject ourselves to God's rule, unless we trust the Giver of all good gifs, we will end up in despair.

To make the most of today keep eternity in mind. *21st July 2011*

THE LORD'S HAND IS NOT SHORTENED, THAT IT CANNOT SAVE ... But your sins have hidden His face from you, so that He will not hear. Isaiah 59:1-2. *22nd July 2011*

READY TO SPEAK? ALWAYS BE READY TO GIVE A DEFENSE TO everyone who asks you a reason for the hope that is in you, with meekness and fear. 1 Peter 3:15. "God has a way of flushing us out of our quiet little places and when He does, we must be ready to speak for Him." To be silent about the Saviour and His salvation is a dreadful Sin of Omission. *23rd July 2011*

CHAPTER SIX
THE BEST ROLE MODELS - MODEL CHRIST

MESSAGE, He who dwells in the shelter of the Most High will abide in the shadow of the Almighty. Psalm 91:1-2, 14-16.

Bugita Mission, Relationship with God (Obuzale, Oruganda, Enkoragana)

This message is about to advise, to counsel, to warn, and to uplift: God is not a Christian, Acts 11:25-26. Our God is a Creator, all Powerful, Loving Father. God is seeking your relationship. When you have relationship with the creator He will trust you. rely on you, tell you His secret, will send you places and trials will come to you.

We are in the last days, Evil days, Believers, know how to scratch for yourself; youth keep yourselves Holy, pastors do not put yourself above everybody. judging, condemning, lying, gossiping, and or rumour mongering. 23rd July 2011

WALK THE WALK, LET NO ONE DESPISE THEIR YOUTH, BUT be an example to the believers in word, in conduct, in love in spirit, in faith and in purity. 1 Timothy 4:12. Talk the talk, but do not walk the walk, anyone can talk a good game but actually performing well is far more difficult; therefore, we please God when our Walk matches our Talk. *24th July 2011*

REPENT, TURN TO GOD, AND DO WORKS BEFITTING, repentance. Acts 26:20. Repentance does not mean just nodding your head politely in agreement with God, and completely continuing the same way we were going, but to completely "Change your mind."

Do we either conform our desires to the truth or conform the truth to our desires? *25th July 2011*

DO ALL THINGS WITHOUT COMPLAINING AND DISPUTING, that you may become blameless and harmless, children of God without fault. Philippians 2:14-15.

"You are responsible, you've got to make good decisions and show people how things are supposed to be done." This I decided when we were going for market crusades at Kigoyera Open Market and stop over mini-crusades on the way home. "That when we go to minister, people who complain of time, husbands, etc. should not go with us because when we go to serve the Lord we had to completely surrender our time, husbands, and children so that we can give our God acceptable holy offering. "The best role models model Christ." God's Heart, Revelations 3:19. *26th July 2011*

REPENTANCE RESTORES AND RENEWS OUR INTIMACY WITH THE LORD.

As many as I love, I rebuke and chasten. Therefore be zealous and repent. Revelation 3:19. *27th July 2011*

JONATHAN CAUSED DAVID TO SWEAR AGAIN, BECAUSE HE loved him: for he loved him as he loved his own soul. 1 Samuel 20:17. A friend is the first person who comes in when the whole world has gone out. *28th July 2011*

CHAPTER SEVEN
MANAGING PROBLEMS POSITIVELY

"He Turns Scars Into Stars!!!"

ROBERT SCHULLER

29TH - 31ST JULY 2011

TWELVE PRINCIPLES OF MANAGING PROBLEMS POSITIVELY, taken from Tough Times Never Last, But Tough People Do. by Robert Schuller.

One, Do not underestimate, the Lord turned my scars into Stars, when I played my problems down and prayed up; this lifted up my Faith in Him. I may not be getting AS and BS, but I am Passing.

Two, don't exaggerate the problem. At times when you have a problem, the best way to Fight is to keep quiet and do not go telling everybody because you want sympathy. Do not compare with others, everyone is different and they get different levels of problems. Hold your problems according to your level of faith, Walk with the Lord, Trust in the Lord.

Play your problem down and Pray it up. Give it to God and give Him a chance to show how the scars can be turned into Stars and give you the ability to cope with the worst that will happen. Stop exaggerating the depth, the length and the breadth of the problem.

Three, do not wait, Schuller wrote "Patience is not a virtue if you sit back and wait for your problem to solve itself." This depends on the Instructions the Lord gives you; for me in the case of Peter, He said Patience pays, when I hanged on the Lord told me "You do not know where Peter is, I am the only one who will bring him back after 20 years.

Also, for Robert, Lord said He will bring him back. Schuller wrote, "If you want to solve your problem, do not wait for somebody else to help you. Tackle it yourself."

Also, this depends on the Lord at times because He uses people to be answers to other people's problems, e.g. sponsorship of tractors to finish the school building.

Four, don't aggravate, do not shift the blame fix the problem. If you have a problem, do not add to it. Do not make your problem worse by aggravating it with self pity, jealousy, cynical, hatred, anger or lack of positive faith in the future.

Five, illuminate IPDE, Identify your problem, Predict how it is going to turn, Decide how you are going to Tackle it, and then Execute to apply the method you know which can solve it.

Six, motivate, "Every obstacle or Problem can be an opportunity;" the kidnapping of Peter and running away of Robert brought me to Dependence on the Lord, Trust in the Lord, Patience, Long Suffering, Faith in the Lord, Praying and waiting,

Focusing on God in Silence not share everything to other people, Hearing from God and Talking to with God.

Seven, bait, in case one asks; "Gertrude how do you build 500m/= School Building in the village?" My answer will be "How do you trap God," We need to set bait for God. Abraham took his only son to offer him on Mt, Moriah , avid sang Praises to God, Solomon gave such a big offering ever given and asked only Wisdom, Mordecai saved the king's life when he gave a report to the king, Esther obeyed her uncle's instructions and did not disclose her race, the Zerepath woman built a beautiful room for Elisha, Abigail ran with provision to King David and saved her people from slaughter.

Eight, date, do not let age be a factor; starting something new at 50 or 60 may be just what you need. I left a government job when I was 51, it was a determination, I asked myself many questions, since I started working, I was working in high offices with many privileges like a free house in prestigious area, big building, free medical and at times free meals on Cabinet Meeting days. Not until I found out that I was a boss of my own and employer of so many people, then I was satisfied.

Nine, sublimate, every problem is loaded with possibilities. You can turn your mountain into a gold mine. Every time one door closes, another one will Open. Every adversity or adversary holds within it the seed of an undeveloped possibility. God uses life's bruises if we surrender them to Him. When you cannot eliminate the problem, but can sublimate it and turn the stumbling block into a stepping stone.

Ten, now dedicate, most people fail, not because they lack intelligence, ability, opportunity or talent but because they haven't given their problem all they have. The positive approach has always attracted the positive support from friends I have known a long time as well as people I have never known before.

Eleven, communicate, pray, ask God questions, and listen for His answers. Be honest when you ask Him for advice.

Twelve, insulate, we need to insulate ourselves from statements, as well as negative climates of General economy, the whole world may feel the pinch or bite of poor economy, but as children of God that does not affect us. Our God is above the economy or world crises, He can provide over and above, where everybody is under, and He will keep you above every circumstance. *1st August 2011*

CHAPTER EIGHT
DUO NGIKUHAIRE, I HAVE GIVEN YOU DOUBLE

THE RIGHTEOUS SHOULD CHOOSE his friends carefully Proverbs 12:26., True friends are like Diamonds, precious and rare. *2nd August 2011*

LEVERAGE AND EXALTATION, BY PASTOR SERWADDA, Leverage, to be exemplary (Kurabibwaho/Kosorobyameans), e.g. when all people are only allowed to use left hand roadside, but when a President and other dignitary's convoys come they are allowed to use the wrong side of the road

God is going to leverage some people for His glory like Joseph who was a slave who had no right at all in the land of Egypt, but when the Lord leveraged him, he became a Prime Minister. Mordecai, the Jew, a captive from Israel who could not be considered for any good position except to be a palace guard, was leveraged to become a Prime Minister of Persia and Median Empire, as was Queen Esther his niece.

Leverage and exaltation comes only from the Lord. *3rd August 2011*

So NEEPU and CIS are surrounded like a dot in the middle of the ocean of idolatries as was Israel was surrounded by allied armies. I remembered the film I saw of king Solomon where he fought the Egyptian allied forces, he told his army to shine their shields until they shined like mirrors and positioned them over the hill facing early morning sunrise, between them was a cliff. When the Egyptian army came, the Israel Army turned their shields towards the sun and blinded the Egyptian army who ended falling off a cliff. Therefore, we are going to shine our shields of faith and face them to the allied idol worshippers around us and let them drive over the cliff.

When Moses and Israelites were leaving Egypt when they reached on the way they were surrounded by mountains north and south, the Red Sea in the east and Egyptian army chasing them from the west. The Israelites were stuck in the middle having nowhere to turn, until the Lord asked Moses to rise his stuff against the Red Sea, it parted and made away for them to pass on the dry land. So, that is how the Lord is going to make NEEPU and CIS pass through the Red Sea.

After prayer, I asked the Lord to talk to me, at random I opened my Bible to Isaiah 43:15-17 reading the same lines I was praying, Amazing. Also, the Holy Spirit asked me to read Isaiah 60, where the Lord has led me several years to read the same Chapter.

A question came to me "What causes you to Fear God and makes you wonder?" *4th August 2011*

FIRST, WHAT CAUSES ME TO FEAR GOD IS WHEN I SEE HIS CREATION. In the sky he made The Moon, the Sun and myriads of Stars of every shape, colour, size, set up and grouping, e.g. Orion, Jupiter, and the Milky Way with all the clusters. The Earth He created, land mass divided by oceans, seas, lakes, rivers, streams and creeks; great mountains and whatever they contain, valleys, forests plains, and deserts.

The second cause is how He created man and hid his thoughts in hearts. Even if one is sharing a bed you may find his thoughts far away, they are sharing the bed but their thoughts are different.

The third cause is how God hid Himself that people cannot familiarize Him. Human beings are familiar animals, if you do not give him a gap, he will try to be equal with you even if the difference is so big, he or she will want to get around you and find where to start.

The fourth cause is John 3:16, I wonder how God gave His only begotten son to come and suffer in the hands of men he created He Himself. *5th August 2011*

I WOKE UP WONDERING HOW I WAS GOING TO HAVE Fellowship with the Lord; as I was coming out of the bathroom, I felt that I had to continue interceding for a woman.

I started by worshiping God, laid my head back on the pillow as usual how I worship the Lord, til I go myself to sleep. It is so wonderful all my being gets into motion of worship. As I was in the middle, the Lord took over and started telling me great and mighty things concerning my walk and love for Him. I kept marveling because they were too deep, too high, too wide to fathom they were beyond human understanding.

The Lord mention to me that each person of God who served Him had, and still is having, a special name the Lord calls him/her. After He said. "Shobal," I wanted to know the meaning of the name. He said it is a secret name between Him and me, persecutor of ... I saw a laptop closing and I asked the meaning of that. He said people used to read or write books, after reading or writing do not they close it. Now it is a computer age most people are using computers, then He said, "I have closed the book, laptop I have been reading."

The Lord talked up to 7.00am and I was still listening asking Him a question here and there, I woke up, got my laptop, as He instructed me that I should write quickly what He has told me. In the process of writing I wanted to read where He said in Revelation that 'I will give you My own new name. Immediately I opened the Bible to look for it in Rev. 3, not knowing exactly which verse, but straight were my eyes on Rev. 3:8-13. Great is thy Faithfulness, O! Lord!!!

Duo Ngikuhaire, I have given you Double, this is a Word He mentioned to me, as I rolled out of bed to go the second time to the bathroom again, He said go and write these words before you forget them.

Again, in the office as I was sharing with Clare I opened the Bible in Haggai my eyes went straight to Haggai 2:6-9.

Breath, another question came from the Lord: How do you get the breath you take? *8th August 2011*

CHAPTER NINE
THE UNIVERSE IS FULL OF THE PRESENCE OF GOD

THE WHOLE UNIVERSE is full of the presence of God. The Bible tells us He is: Omnipresence, He is everywhere at one time, He fills the universe. 2) Omniscient He knows everything because He is the one who created everything. 3) Omnipotent, He has no beginning Alpha and No End Omega.

We do not see the movement of the air we breathe it enters even in closed doors. Imagine in the airplane, all windows air sealed, in big liners on the ocean, you find yourself breathing. The breath we take in and breath out repels anything around when you are sleeping, bugs, snakes, etc. cannot enter your nostrils.

The breath we take is life giving breath, no one knows where it comes from or where it goes. When a person dies you find all people around still breathing and only the dead one's life giving breath is cut off. This breath sustains environment around, even buildings. If you leave a house empty for some time without occupying it, its surroundings will start dilapidating start losing life, but if there is a human being even if it is a mad man the plants around will become live e.g. there was a mad man who lived on Entebbe Road. Also, my plantation at the farm when one worker was living in the house everything was growing green, the moment when he left the avocado trees, the bananas started growing weak until there were no more health plants. In a farm because of workers who work there or animals' breath is important to the farm. Man has a Life of God in him, Ecclesiastes 3:11, He put Eternity into our Hearts. *10th August 2011*

CHAPTER TEN
SISTER JUDI ZAK

THIS IS a great joy to talk about my sister, friend, mentor Sis. Judi Zak. I met Sister Judi in 1993 in Lancaster, California at Sis. Agnes' Ministry. At that time, she was one of the Board of Directors of All Nations International. Sis. Agnes called her and said "Sis Judi, I want you to help Gertrude" from that time Sister Judi adopted me and 4 biological war orphaned children, 10 AIDS orphan children of my siblings and a school of 400 children with 25 Staff members. In 2004 she introduced me to Judy Hellmich who joined us to share the vision.

Sister Judy filled in many gaps: A humble maidservant of the Lord!!! Mother and grandmother, sister, Friend, mentor, teacher, great thinker, Super Planner, great manager, great advisor, great Organizer, an Orator, wonderful companion, host and encourager.

Sis Judi was a great co-coordinator. With her expertise we started a sponsoring program in 2006 for the orphans in my rural poor district in Uganda where a number of both orphans and poor children in Nyamabuga Primary School were being sponsored. She organized a plan to get animals for the orphans to enhance their welfare.

The words we talk and speak can lead to life or death, Sis Judi spoke words of wisdom and deeper knowledge to the extent that every time she wondered that she had much information concerning the Kingdom.

Sis Judi's last conversation with me on 14th August when we talked for half an hour was asking me "have you staked the farmland and was giving me instructions how stake the land for the Lord." That the Lord spoke to her concerning the piece of the 100 acres of the farm land that it is a Base for the Lord not only for Uganda but for the whole continent of Africa.

Her last message to me was on 14th August, it was a prophecy about the "Shaking and the Lord's Coming."

There are songs which are sang to bring joy or destruction., Sis Judi's heart was full of heaven, her song was 'Open the Eyes of my heart Lord, I want to see you,' to see you high and lifted up ... whenever I asked her to sing.

There are friends one can make who are useful or useless, Sis Judi made useful friends.

All the friends she introduced me were meaningful, serious, loving, down to earth and like jewels. She had a good selection of friends.

There are children who can lead to joy or sorrow; when Sis Judi introduced me to her dear children, they took me as one of their family members and started helping their mum in the great work God was doing in Uganda, Africa to win souls for Christ. This also has been her great excitement, whenever I gave her a report from missions.

There are jobs which are open for blessing or are devil's snares and traps. Sis Judi every year in March – April took leave from her job to accompany me from State to State to raise funds for the village school construction; we started in 2007, now almost complete, and to support the mobile evangelization in the rural areas of Uganda. All this was her great joy. There were journeys and trips we took back and forth internally and externally, but there is a journey which we will take, and we shall not return. Sis Judi, walked, talked, lived, and sang of that journey and prepared herself for it. The journey of no return comes like a thief; many times it takes people unaware.

ARE YOU PREPARING FOR THIS JOURNEY?

21st August 2011
The Call, by Rick Joyner, continued, the quality of relationship will be determined by the quality of communication, and any relationship that does not have continuing communication is dying relationship.

One who speaks in tongues edifies himself, but one who prophecies edifies the church 1 Corinthians 14:3-4. The scriptures encourage us to "especially" seek the gift of Prophesy.

The Lord told Rick that "I am the Saviour and I am the Judge. First I must reveal my Judgment to my own Household. I am the Judge, but it is better for you to judge yourself so that I will not have to judge you." *17th September 2011*

HAD A DREAM ABOUT THE BANK, BANK DOCUMENTS, THERE was another person a young man was involved in the same Bank, we were given same instruction to access it. The Young man got so active to access it, but for me I was still watching and waiting. Its colours were Green & White.

I woke up and went to sleep, it continued. I woke up again the Lord started to speak to me: about the African Continent Bank, about the Position in that Bank, and its greatness on the continent. The Lord going to employ the staff of that bank. The Lord spoke to me about the great treasures He put on the continent and He mentioned those who stole the riches of Africa, that He is going to bring those who stole those riches begging.

He told me about the high calling where everyone will be dumb founded. The 5 + 1 jet will make one plane and about flying all over Africa executing His Business, that no one will question academic qualifications.

About the set up He put in Clare and Emma and the great wisdom He has provided in His close relationship and communication we are going to share.

Sis. Judi's calling and the spiritual impact she has on Africa Continent. That Sis Judi's decision her body to be brought to Africa was revealed to her and that her children will be involved in the Ministry. The Lord asked me to write Sis Judi's prophesy to prove all this what He has decided to do.

Judi's prophesy for Gertrude, the Lord takes great pleasure in calling you to the impossible, asking you to see the invisible Victory, to see the invisible Kingdom, He is calling you to do the outrageous! Carry on in His Great Grace, His great Goodness & His great Glory, magnifying His Name and Glorifying Him on the earth. He's waited a long time, to find a servant like you! *18th September 2011*

Judi Zak and Kabatalemwa with grandchildren

Judi Helmich and Teresa Skinner with Kabatalemwa

CHAPTER ELEVEN
HOW DO I KEEP FROM FEELING SO SMALL

AGAIN THE LORD started to speak to me: He talked of 45 days of preparation, He talked of 40 years of Moses' Preparation and He talked of 40 years of Israelites in the wilderness and He talked how the enemy does not give up, That people will continue bluffing, despising, and challenging but victory continues then He concluded how people have failed to understand me even, the children in my own house. *25th July 2011*

I GOT A MESSAGE ABOUT A CANDIDATE. WHEN PEOPLE ARE about to sit for examination there is Special Time of Preparation for the examination. There has to be revision of all what one was taught, there has to be special group discussions. At that time, one reads nearly each and every topic of the subjects because one will never know where the question will come from. Therefore, the question is, if the candidate of this world Takes Time to Prepare for his other worldly exam, how is it for one to Prepare for the Final Exam for Eternity?

Many people have taken it for kicks or games, they say I still have time, I will prepare when I will see I am about to die, etc. A dream in March 2006 when I was in CA in an Examination room. *23rd September 2011*

THE LORD SPOKE TO BRO RICK JOYNER SAYING "MANY people fall when My Spirit touches them. The time for falling is over. You must learn to stand when My Spirit moves. If you do not stand when My Spirit moves, He cannot use you. The heathen should fall before me, but I need for My people to stand so that I can use them."

About trials, The strength and effectiveness of a trap is determined by its elasticity.

The strong mature wine is determined by the length of time it takes to be brewed.

The food fit for the king's dish depends on time it takes on slow fire.

The Olympic medalist marathon runner is determined by the time spent practicing

Pride of false humility, Inadequacy, inefficient, inability, unworthiness, incompetency. Bro Rick pleaded in the presence of the Lord "but your presence is so overwhelming. How do I keep from feeling so small when I'm close to you like this?"

The Lord answered: "You are small, but you must learn to abide in My Presence without looking at yourself. You will not be able to hear from Me or speak for Me if you are looking at yourself. You will always be inadequate. You will always be unworthy for what I call you to do but it will never be your adequacy or worthiness that causes Me to use you. You must stop looking at your own unworthiness and look to my righteousness. When you are used, it is because of who I AM, not who you are."

The Lord told Bro Rick that "This is the anger I felt towards Moses when he started to complain about how inadequate he was. This only reveals that you are looking to yourself more than to Me which is the main reason why I am able to use so few of My people for what I desire to do. This false humility is actually a form of the pride that caused the fall of man. Adam and Eve began to feel inadequate and that they needed to be more than I had made them to be."

This refers to the message I got on 28th July 2010 when I was traveling to USA for the Funeral of Sis Agnes.

When the Sovereignty of God overshadows our incompetencies, (Obusobozi/Enkora ya Ruhanga kuswekerra obutesobora bwaitu).

Many times one has looked at his or her inadequacy of height, fluency, age, academics, income, looks, race, etc. and said God cannot or would have used me if I had that height like so and so or if I had good academic papers to show, or if my speech was fluent to express or explain issues precisely and accurately, if I was young enough maybe old enough, like Jeremiah's complaint about his inadequacy of speech and age, Jeremiah 1:4-8. Others say if I had enough money, I would go here and there to serve the Lord, if I had good looks, or they plead to the Lord of their inadequacy of a race.

We look at Mordecai the Jew, who looked at God despite of his race and situation, a captive in a foreign land. He kept looking at the adequacy of His creator and God made him a Prime Minister in the whole empire of Persia and Medes, even though Haman the Agagite tried to put pressure on him to accept his plight of a captive and of Jew, but he refused the False Humility and looked at the adequacy, sovereignty or ability of God, Esther 3:5-6.

Joseph and Jacob often the inadequacy of worshipping the Lord shows up as weakness. Joseph had to go through hard circumstances when his brothers tried to kill him then threw him in a pit, he was sold to the Ishmaelites, when Potiphar's wife tried to rape him and he was thrown in prison, Genesis 39:20-23. The Sovereignty, competency, and adequacy of the Lord covered the inadequacy and unworthiness of Joseph; the Lord used him to save Egypt and the family of his father from famine.

Sarah's inadequacy kept her without a child for 90 years which caused her to offer her Egyptian slave girl to her husband which was an abomination. It is unheard of a respected wife, even at this time offering to share her husband with a house girl. Sarah was desperate for a child. Then the Lord in His sovereignty came and covered her inadequacy at 90 years of age and gave her Isaac to fulfill His promise. Later Hagar became a thorn in her flesh, to the extent of asking Abraham to chase away the slave woman with her child.

Hannah, the wife of Elkanah, she had no children and she was tormented by her co-wife Penninah who used to taunt and provoke her day after day because she had no children.

Even though Elkanah promised her that she was to him more than ten sons, but she really wanted a child from her own womb. After pouring her heart to the Lord without putting her petition to the High Priest the Lord used His adequacy over her inadequacy and gave her Samuel who became a great Judge of Israel.

We also have David who killed Goliath with one smooth stone. We have Daniel who was thrown in a Lion's Den and the Lord closed the lions' mouths. We have Shadrach, Meshach and Abednego who walked in a furnace and the Lord walked with them there.

DO NOT SAY "I HAVE TO HUMBLE MYSELF"

Do not say "I have to humble myself" much more so that the Lord will use me effectively, this is False Humility. The Lord told me on 3rd October 2010, "Be Yourself, Be Normal, Be Natural." Surrender to the Lord all your inabilities, incompetencies and unworthiness then Lord will cloth you with His Ability, Competency and Adequacy and use you. *2nd October 2011*

THE CALL, BY RICK JOYNER CONTINUED, THESE POINTS OR tips I marked them for remembrance in my walk with the Lord because these people had encounters with the Lord. The Lord allowed Rick to meet some Patriarchs who answered many questions he was asking the Lord.

Lot told Rick that he was silent in Sodom and Gomorah and many people perished. Are you also going to keep quiet so that people perish and you save only your soul? The power of the Holy Spirit convicts us of sin, and the Holy Spirit is released by the Spoken Word of God. If those people who know the Lord do not arise, there will be many more like Sodom very soon. Already, New Orleans was devastated by hurricane Katrina, Indonesia was flooded with a Tsunami, Haiti had a destructive Earthquake, part Japan was ruined by a Tsunami, Tornadoes and Hurricanes in the USA, etc. What else is next?

You must seek His judgments every day and make them known on the earth to the perishing. The messages of judgment must go forth in Words, the Holy Spirit's Words, but the Words must be Spoken in order for Him to anoint them. Righteousness and Justice are the foundation of God's Throne. The Lord always extends mercy before Judgment and His Mercy will save many.

The Lord allowed Rick to meet Jonah, and he shared with Rick that: "Do not seek the presence of the Lord but abide in His presence daily." True. Jonah told Rick that the Church is running from the presence of the Lord to the activities they call Ministry, so that it can trade with the World seeking the treasures of the

Sea as I did. In the end I was thrown out and the monster swallowed me. Some churches are also going to be swallowed by the beast which is going to come out of the sea, Revelations.

Never become proud because of your visions, this will always lead you to fall. *5th October 2011*

CHAPTER TWELVE
THE PRESENCE OF GOD

MESSAGE, The day one dies is better than the day he is born, Ecclesiastes 7:1. Why? The answer was found in Ecclesiastes 7:8 That Finishing or end of a matter is better than its beginning.

For me, my explanation is that when one is born, he has just entered in World where he has to play roles and meet challenges. When one is born few people know due to the fact that he or she is not announced, that he has been born on that day or month, except in the cases like a few Celebrities famous with this internet computer age.

So, after playing roles, passing examinations and failing some, plus achievements - one is brought into the limelight where many people will know who he or she was and will give their Eulogy as a good review or a bad one. One day on a TV series where Mr A died and Mr B his friend was asked to speak at his funeral, after clearing his throat he said.

"The bereaved family, all dignitaries-protocol observed and, fellow mourners: I am not going to mince words, Mr A was such a dishonest person, a thief, a liar, etc. I know the neighborhood is going to rest now because his life was a mess. Many times, people like telling lies that: 'O, Mr A was such a good man, may his soul rest in peace.' You are also a liar if you are saying that so better keep quiet and say nothing, at least they will not quote you."

When one is born, they are not yet known as a thief, rapist, a Pastor, Pope or President, but the day he dies he has stepped on many people's toes or lifted many people from the ground, caused much grief or happiness to families and served in many hierarchies. *7th October 2011*

I WENT TO THE BANK TO LOOK FOR THE LOAN TO CONTINUE finishing the school but was disappointed when the Business Banker asked so many questions which did not make sense to me. I was so annoyed I left in protest and repented to the Lord, why at this time I did not continue trusting him, who has led me this far.

The Call, by Rick Joyner continued: Intimacy will bring about "Blessings," but "pursuing blessings" will not always bring intimacy. Whatever or whoever is exposed to the manifested presence of God begins to absorb the very material matter of God, Exodus 34:29-35, when Moses came back from Mt Sinai. *7th October 2011*

MY PRECEDENT PRAYER, INDEPENDENCE DAY, OUR LORD loved us so much, He left Heaven and came to save us. He gave up His position, glory and prestige to come and die in agony on the cross. Humbly I ask, Lord, let me love you as you loved me.

Whoever comes to Him, He embraces him. Jesus does not want to send Anyone away. When you come to Him, He will stretch His hands towards you. He does not see into your inadequacy, incapabilities, lack, incompetence, or unworthiness. He sees you as a child and He suffered for you on the cross. Humbly I ask, Here I come Lord, let me see your glory.

When He was on the earth, He saw sickness of the poor people and He wanted to heal them. He opened the blind eyes, He healed the lame, He cleansed the lepers and He rose the dead. Wonderful Jesus, He is still healing all manner of diseases today for those who believes in Him. Humbly I ask, Lord Heal me now spiritually and physically, let me be whole.

Most of all He preached the Good News, the way of Salvation and of His loving heart. Our Lord did not only live a good life, He also told people the way to live, the way to go to heaven and His loving kindness. Humbly I ask, Lord, let me be obedient and take your Word to all Nations.

But evil jealous people hated Him so much, in His kind healing hands they drove nails.

Jealous is a terrible evil, it blinds people to the extent of murder. Our Lord was murdered for the good deeds which led the Pharisees and other religious people to a criminal act.

Humbly I ask, Help me to forgive these evil jealous people at present and in future.

On the shameful cross, they crucified Him with anger, and drove nails in His hands.

The cross where our Lord was hanged was so rough. He did not deserve to die such a criminal death, but He accepted to die as a criminal in my place.

Humbly I ask, Precious Jesus, let me always repent whenever I remember that Cross You Hanged On For Me. For His kindness and much love for that's how He chose to die for me, got Himself killed in my place. Humbly I ask, My God! My God! Have Mercy on me, and spare me from Judgment which is coming for those who denied you. Amen. *9th October 2011*

PRAYER, LORD, I REPENT OF WHEN YOU ASKED ME TO ASK what I want after going through the preparation of 45 days on 7th October 2010. I wrote down, 18 points which I feel are really good, but after reading Bro. Tommy Tenny's book, the 18 points condensed into 9, which I take now instead of 18.

I will ask no more blessing – I want you the Blesser
I will ask no more gifts – I want you the giver
I will ask no more healing – I want you the healer
Let me not seek revival – but seek you the reviver
I would like to be excited about only YOU God
I would like to be a woman after Your Heart
Lord, give me the Grace to be willing to die in order to see your Glory
May I be that lamb on the Altar to be killed in order to see God's Face
May I take off my eyes from the Toys- but focus on the purpose of my calling.
May you Lord show me where you're going to break open, so that I can position myself.

The greatest blessing does not come from God's hand, it comes from His Face, an intimate relationship when you finally see Him and know Him, you have come to the source of all power. Amen. *10th October 2011*

THE GOD CHASERS BY TOMMY TENNY, IN THE OLD Testament, when a person refused to show you his face, he was deliberately turning away from you, that is Shunning. So is God. Bro Tenny says God is tired of screaming instructions at the

Church; He wants to guide us with His Eye. He is tired of correcting us through public censure.

If you seek His face what you get is His favour. We have long enjoyed the omnipresence of God, but now we are experiencing brief moments of visitation of His manifest presence. It causes every hair to stand up on end, and it makes demonic forces to flee and run. If we are not going to sing of God's glory in the streets of the city, markets in the villages and Camps in tea plantations, then He will raise up a generation that is nonreligious and uninhibited and reveal His glory to them.

The Presence of God is a difference between the Omnipresence of God and the Manifest Presence of God. Omnipresence of God refers to God being everywhere all the time. He is that "particle" in the atomic nucleus that physicists cannot see and can only track. God is in a bar, is on the street, He is in Hospital, Prison, Asylum, and He is everywhere.

The Manifest Presence of God God is everywhere all the time, there are also times when He concentrates His being into "the manifest presence of God" when this happens, there is a strong sense and awareness that God Himself has entered this room. There are also specific periods of time when He is "here" more than "there." For divine reasons God chooses to concentrate, or reveal, Himself more strongly in one place than another, or more at one time than another. If my people, which are called by my name, shall humble themselves, and pray, and seek my face, and turn from their wicked ways; then will I hear from heaven, and will forgive their sin, and will heal their land. 2 Chronicles 7:14. If they are already His people, What other level of "Him" are they to "seek?'" You can be God's child and not have His favour, much as an earthly child would be in disfavor but not be disowned.

People will come as soon as they hear that the Presence of God is in the place. When HE comes you won't need any Advertisements on bill boards, newspapers, on radio or Television. All you need is God and people will come from far and near on any given night or day, e.g. Katherine Khulman, Mary Etter, and Wigglesworth crusades.

People used to fly from Europe and Canada to go for the Presence of God. *10th October 2011*

CHAPTER THIRTEEN
SEEK THE REVIVER - NOT THE REVIVAL

MESSAGE, The people stood far off and Moses drew near into the thick darkness where God was, Exodus 20:18-21
 Question, Why God into the thick darkness?
 Answer, God does not look at the flesh. Only dead men see His Face, the secret path to His presence. Exodus 33:17, 18-20, smoke and thick darkness are a curtain that protects man from seeing God's Face.
 You cannot walk with God in flesh and live, but you will "Die" along the way "Enoch" could not return home, Gen. 5:21-24.

IT IS TIME TO SEEK THE REVIVER, AND NOT THE REVIVAL.

We need to Date God giving Him days and times for fun and games, Church Clubs where people go for "thrills and chills" is over. God is tired of us wanting to get our thrills from Him without putting on the ring of commitment. God is still looking for His bride not a girl friend; one who will stick with Him. We need God to deal with us to a point where we will be forced to redefine the purpose as to what is means to be Saved. *11th October 2011*

SINCE 28TH OCTOBER I CONTINUED PRAYING AND repenting on behalf of the President and Uganda. After hearing many people wishing what happened in Libya on 20th October 2011 should happen to the President and this nation I was so much grieved and decided to continue the interceding which started on 23rd October. I removed all pillows and slept flat on my face, then on 1st November started using the Bible as my pillow and requested the Lord to Saturate His Word in my system like when you place a cursor to copy in Excel, there is a border which saturates the field you want to copy.

My Prayer, Lord, as I embrace this Bible it is your Word, Your word is You, Yourself. In the beginning was the Word, and the Word was with God, and the Word was God. John 1:1. Your Word is Wisdom, Understanding and Knowledge itself. You said that Wisdom is found by those who fear the Lord, Job 28; and Understanding is found by those who run from Evil, Proverbs 8, Let me live on your Word, walk on it, think of it. Let it be Food and Drink for my Spirit and Soul and let it saturate my whole system as long as I live. Lord, whenever I am about to say a wrong word or make a wrong statement let my tongue hang at the roof of my mouth. Whenever I am about to take any action or walk into any enemy's trap or snare put me on pause until that situation has passed. When a wrong wish, thought, desire, anticipation, expectation or imagination occurs in my mind and tries to derail me away from your righteous ways let my mind be suspended for a moment and allow me focus on you. Amen. *9th November 2011*

MEN KNOW HOW TO OBTAIN FOOD FROM THE SURFACE OF the earth, while underneath there is fire. They dam up streams of water and pan the gold. But though men can do all these things, they do not know where to find Wisdom and Understanding. for it is hid from all eyes of mankind, even the sharp-eyed bird in the sky cannot discover it. And God surely knows where it is to be found, for he looks throughout the whole earth under all the heavens. He knows where Wisdom is and declares it to all who will listen. and this is what he says to all mankind: "Look, to fear the Lord is true wisdom, to forsake evil is real understanding." Job 28:1-28. *12 November 2011*

CHAPTER FOURTEEN
WHERE DID EVIL COME FROM?

PEOPLE ASK Where Did the Evil Come From, Especially in Heaven?

Wow! I received at 6.15am, evil lived in heaven, it coexisted with Righteousness, until when it looked for habitation, where to breed and found Lucifer. As Righteousness cannot share the same habitation with evil, one had to leave.

In the Divine, Spiritual and Natural laws there is no way one can judge good and evil without comparison. There has to be two entities. To be able to find out a fake currency note, there has to be a genuine note. However, time evil matured and had found an abode to inhabit and began to claim.

By then Lucifer was the most beautiful creature God had ever made. Then evil entered him and he desired to be the most high and wanted to set his throne above the one of the Almighty. After evil getting a foot hold in Lucifer evil pursued 1/3 of the angels who also agreed with him.

Transfer of spirits, when you hang around a good person you also become good, when you hang around an evil person you take after the same character.

All along our Father knew the plot of Lucifer because He is

Omniscient, God knows everything. At this point He threw satan out of Heaven. satan, the devil goes before God, cause he knows there-heaven used to be his home until when he was thrown out. satan went among the sons of God.

God had a short conversation with him: God asked satan: "From where do you come? Have you considered my Servant Job? For there is no one like him on the earth ... satan asked God does Job fear God for nothing? Have you not made a hedge about him and his house, and all that he has on every side?

You have blessed the works of his hands. The Lord said behold all that he has is in your power, only do not forth your hand on him. So satan departed from the presence of the Lord. Job 1:6-12. Again, there was a day when the sons of God came to present themselves ... and satan also came among them to present himself before the Lord.

The Lord asked satan: From where do you come? Have you considered my Servant Job? For here is no one like him on the earth .... although you incited Me against him without cause."

Satan answered: Skin for skin! Yes, all that man has he will give for his life. However, put forth you hand now and touch his bone and his flesh, he will curse you to your face. The LORD said to satan behold he is in your power, only spare his life. Satan went out from the presence of the Lord and smote Job with sores and boils from the sole of his foot to the crown of his head. Job 2:1-7.

The third time satan is cited in heaven is in 1 Kings said he saw the Lord sitting on His Throne and all the hosts of heaven standing on his right and on His left. The Lord asked who will entice Ahab to go and fall at Ramoth-gilead? One said this, another said that. A spirit then came forth and stood before the Lord and said I will go and entice him. The Lord said: How? And the spirit said I will go out and be a deceiving spirit in the mouths of the Prophets. The Lord said you are to entice him and then prevail. Go and do so, 1 Kings 22:19-22. *13th November 2011*

Children Singing

Dancing Ugandan Traditional Dances

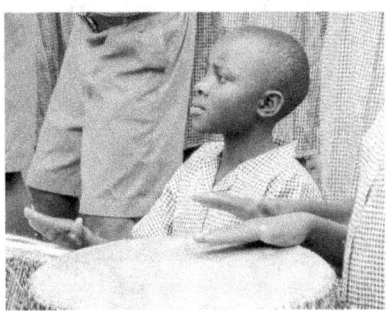

Playing the drum

Outside of second classroom built

Students in classroom

CHAPTER FIFTEEN
I AM CHRIST WHO CALLED YOU

MESSAGE, after 56 hours waiting on the Lord, asking Him to heal me of the thyroid.
 I am not sitting, I am not standing, I am not walking but I am just here. I have given you the iPad, it's your gift which you will be using on the job I have given you.
 I am Christ who called you. There is no any person who will get what I have put in your hands!!!

Kanabanatanlenemwana!! (x3)
Ine hanavenu trusten youn!! (x3)
Gonodin yourn an crenatorn insin then en onenun whonmun hansin conolledin youn!!!

Sincesin the en Worldin bengunin, we nin hanavun neneveran pronoduncin an wonrriniyan linken youn!!!

Kanabanatanalenemwana Inin vanaluen youn son munchin, thana its whyanin Inin hanavun takenin tinmun toon trainin youn forn sunchin an longin tinmun.

Inin hanvun runin within youn an worldin Marathonin.
t....ime t..o tr...ain y..ou fo..r s...uch a lo...ng ti...me. I h...ave r...un w..ith u a wor...ld M..ar..ath..on.

People think in human terms, but this is in Spiritual terms. *13th October 2011*

PRIDE, GOD IS A CREATOR OF CHARACTERISTICS:

- Mountain Goat - God gave it a determination how it leaps on sharp cliffs,
- Wild Ox - Rebel you cannot tame it or make it plow your field,
- Ostrich - Stupid but has speed, does not care for its babies,
- Horse - Brave and fearless, in war does not turn back in front of ...
- Eagle - Wise and watchful, Job 39.

The Lord Humiliates the proud and haughty with a glance; tread down the wicked where they stand. knock them into the dust and stone face them in death. As I was about to write on the verse Saddam and Gadaffi the Holy Spirit said: "Do not write their names in my Book." Job 40:12-13. *29th October 2011*

MESSAGE, THE HOLY SPIRIT LED ME TO OPEN PSALMS 136 to 139 crashed on me. In Psalm 137:5 I made a promise: if forget you Lord, may my arms be pulled out of their sockets. May my tongue cling to the roof of my mouth. If do not remember you and not exalt you Lord. Job 41:11. The Lord says: who has given or lent me that I should repay him? Whatever is under the whole heaven is mine. Wisdom again I was led to read in Proverbs 8 which relates to Job 28:27-28 where the Holy Spirit led to read on 12th October 2011. *5th November 2011*

I WAS WOKEN UP BY A LOT OF NOISE OF CHANTING AS IT WAS a day of Idi Adhuha, the day of killing animals. I heard the Spirit telling me that I start praying against that spirit. I prayed and sealed the outer space and claimed that this is going to be the last Idi Adhuha in East African Muslims. I repeated 5 precedent Prayer with the Matthew 18:18, Revelation 12:11, Daniel 11:32 and Ecclesiastes 3:11.

As I prayed, I was worshiping the Lord. I remembered the tiny insect which has a home in my Bible. It makes me wonder, it is smaller than a Full stop. When I keep watching its movement it jumps across the page; this puts me to think so much about the greatness of the Creator. I ask myself where does this insect breed, what does it eat, how does it produce its own kind, where does it draw its energy especially, to fly or jump across the pages?

How is its digestive system, where is its heart, what about its productive life does it lay eggs or produce babies, how a big are the babies? Then I remembered the Blue Whale I saw at the Pacific Ocean Aquarium at Long Beach Los Angeles. There is no creature bits it in size on the planet, it feeds each day on 8 tons of tiny fish called krill, who supplies all that and how many blue whales are living in Pacific Ocean? Who keeps their constant supply? God you are awesome.

At times after going through experiences, observing the Creation of God I am shattered and left in awe, I feel like bowing down and worshiping Him, my creator. Especially these days I am experiencing His presence more, closer to Him, and feel in my spirit that His coming is at hand. People should leave everything and come to know Him. He is real!!! *6th November 2011*

THE HOLY SPIRIT LED ME TO READ JOHN 13 ABOUT OUR Lord where He washed His disciple's feet and had His last Supper, this scripture I had read it on 7th November 2010 what a coincidence? I was wondering about how our Lord foretold of the morsel He dipped and gave to Judas, He compared him with Ahithophel, a friend of King David who joined Absolom his son who had rebelled against him ... in 1 Samuel and 1 Kings. Indeed, when Peter asked John to ask Him who was going to betray Him, He dipped the bread and gave it to Judas. *7th November 2011*

CHAPTER SIXTEEN
WITH GOD IS SYNERGY

I WOKE up to pray at 1.00pm. As usual I was talking to the Lord telling Him my life I have lived.

Message, With God is Synergy.

LORD PEOPLE HAVE MOM, FATHER, BROTHERS, SISTERS, aunts, and uncles, I have none.

People have husbands who will cheer them, bring this, that and make them feel happy. I got none. I am living in the house which I rent from a widow, her husband died and left her a beautiful house, at least every month she gets rent. But God gives me money for Rent. People have children who help their parents after educating them, for me at my age I am the one who is helping my big children who would be helping me.

When Peter was 2 was kidnapped and never returned until when he was 24 years; after only one year of his return Robert took off now ten years which makes it 32 years of crying, yearning, longing and strained eyes, always waiting and anticipating of the return of Robert. I have shared in loneliness, longing and sickness.

I have lost the loved ones, my mentor whom I met since January 1989, the ones I counted on so much Sis Agnes died July 17th 2010. Sis Judi who was the Coordinator of NEEPU who fundraised lobbied for sponsorship and all projects of building and my Travel Companion died on 20th August 2011 when I needed her most. When I got Mr. Streoble who sympathized with me to build the school, before he accomplished what he had promised to give me all the funds finish the school he died. *8th November 2011*

AT THIS POINT I CRIED HOT TEARS AND THEN LAUGHED. I asked myself "Does the Lord Love me or Hate me?" And I answered myself that "Neither He hates me nor He Loves me; but He is God, with Him is a Synergy." God Loves me whatsoever I go through.

I reminded the Lord of all what He has been promising me and I said until when Lord. I am getting old. How shall I enjoy of all those promises?

At this point I remembered Sarah, the wife of Abraham, who waited upon Isaac; the Lord promised her until she was 90 years old when she got a baby; a 90 year old woman giving birth? Unheard of!

Then I came to remember Mary, the Mother of our Lord. She was a virgin, the angel came and told her that she was going to have a baby by the Holy Spirit. Mary was confused and disturbed. Later she ran into the highlands to tell her aunt Elizabeth, who called her a blessed lady, Luke 1:30-45. When Mary's time came to give birth of the Holy Child, she could not get a decent place where to deliver, all the Inns were full except a lowly place in a Manger where there were cows and donkeys watching the new born King of kings, Jesus.

The Angel announced the birth of our Lord to the Sheppards, then the armies of heaven were seen singing and glorifying God in the Highest, they came running to look for Him the New Born King. God did not tell rich men and prestigious people in town. After when Jesus was presented to the Temple Simeon mentioned to Mary that "a Sword shall pierce your soul." Again, another episode three kings and astrologers appeared at the home of Joseph, threw themselves worshipping the King of Kings and presented Him with rich gifts. Matthew 2:11. Still Mary wondered.

After the departure of the kings Joseph receives a message escape to Egypt because Herod is seeking to kill the baby who was about a year. Still I think Mary was asking herself about the angel Gabriel, when he appeared to her said this was going to be a Son of God, then can't God protect His child but He tells us to run to Egypt?

With God is Synergy:

2+2 or 2x2 does not make a 4 but remains a 2.
2+1 does not make a 3 But remains a 2.
The things of God are puzzling. *12th April 2010*

THE LORD WOKE ME UP AT THE 11TH HOUR TO PRAY. *11TH November 2011*

WHEN WE REACHED AT RWENZORI TRAVELLERS INN FROM Mweya Safari Lodge I was sharing Room 011 with Dr Ashley Joseph of India who had come to join other Dental Doctors for the exercise of treating the children's teeth at Nyamabuga. *20th November 2011*

CHAPTER SEVENTEEN
YOU ARE THE FORERUNNER

PEOPLE NEED to Intimately know Jesus as a Person and Christ's Message of His Anointing. Let the Church work together to show the world a witness of who Jesus is and not just look for the Signs.

The Lord Spoke to me about the "Forerunner" message. The Lord spoke to my heart that "Do you know Katera Rume?" What does Katera Rume do? I listed the duties Katera Rume does.

Before the suitor goes to introduce himself to the girl's parents, he looks for a person who goes ahead of him to the parents of the girl. This man always knows both families. He is the one who goes to tell the girls side the boy's family back ground of the boys.

I know the suitor, his father and the family back ground. So the Lord was telling me that we are His Forerunners. At one point He raised His voice and said "But people when they are told facts about me they make them a laughing matter and call them a joke."

He said you are My Forerunners. You are to people to tell the World about Me because it is You who know me! You have walked with me! You have talked with me! It is you I have saved!

It is you I have healed! It is you I have fought the battle for! It is you I have carried on my shoulders! It is you I have provided for! It is you who know my Story.

Jesus is the Suitor, you are Forerunner to go and tell His Bride to be who He is!!!

On 3rd December I was preparing a meal for Sis Teresa and Bro Gordon in the kitchen again I heard the Lord saying "John the Baptist, was my forerunner" who said Prepare the Way for the Lord's coming. Now there is no John the Baptist, it is you to tell people about my coming, because it is you who know me. *21st November 2011*

It rained so much, throughout the night till morning, our house flooded, water was coming between the walls, we tried to dry the floors but as it continued raining there was no way how we could dry the floor. At that time the Team came from Hotel Olympia to my House and Sis Lucille as she walked in I was seated at the dining table with Bro Gordon Skinner. As she approached us she slipped and we saw her going down almost hitting her head on sharp edge of a carving, but the hand of the Lord could not let her. She fell right on her back. Bro Gordon and myself just jumped on our feet and grabbed her and started to cancel any injury or hurt on her limbs. The Lord was with us, we helped her up and nothing was wrong with her at all, but the enemy had meant to hurt her. Our God is marvelous.*28th November 2011*

On this day as some guests were with me as we drove

along Kololo Prince Charles Drive Plot 8 at the North Korean Embassy narrating my ordeal of working in the office of Idi Amin. There, the father of Robert was arrested and killed at the Command Post of Iddi Amin which is now the North Korean Embassy. As we drove one brother pointed his video camera to take a view the former Command Post, a North Korean staff spotted us. We drove on and made a u-turn passing again the Embassy to go and take a video on Prince Charles Plot 6 where I lived from 1980 to 1997.

I was sharing the atrocities which were committed there when I was living on that property. As I was explaining, a Korean Ambassador and Tae-kwondo youth paused before us spiting fire. It made matters worse when they saw Americans were the ones videoing their Residency. The Lord made them forget to confiscate the Camera and their focus was on me.

I got courage of a lion and talked to him in affirmative composure. They demanded my identity and I gave them my NEEPUganda visiting card. As they left, we continued with Plot 6, as we came out the guest was so frightened I grabbed her hand and prayed erasing the whole episode out of the Korean's heads and commanding the visiting card to disappear from them and raise no complaint anywhere. We went for lunch at Garden City, still my guest was still shaky about the whole matter, I grabbed her hand and prayed the Lord to make her forget about the incident. She forgot completely and we never talked about it again. 30th November 2011

I WAS PRAYING IN MY HEART THINKING OF MY LANDLORD'S 2 year baby and why she was suffering from the attack of a demon which was coming and trying to strangle her. As I was thinking I heard the screaming, immediately I knew it was from the landlord. Immediately I was filled with the spirit of the Lord, I ran as fast as an Olympic runner across the house and next I climbed the stairs like a mad woman. Found when she was holding the baby who was like dead and she was wailing.

I just grabbed the baby into my hands as the demon was gagging I called for my anointing oil and anointed her and claimed the scriptures on her life. The whole family was gathered helplessly. I stopped the mother to cry. The demon started groaning and I commanded it out, the baby opened her bowels and pooped, opened her eyes and relaxed in my arms, I gave her back to her mother. From that time the demon never attacked her again. *1st December 2011*

SIS TERESA SKINNER HAD LEFT ON THIS EVENING. *7TH December 2011*

CHAPTER EIGHTEEN
CLOSENESS, NEARNESS, INTIMACY

ABOUT FASTING. On this day I wanted to start a fast, but the Lord spoke to my heart and said "The fast does not change God." It is the state of your relationship and intimacy with God. Many people have fasted and prayed but when God saw their hearts were far away from Him. *8th December 2011*

IN MY EARLY MORNING DEVOTIONS, AS I WOKE UP, I HAD A Word in my Heart saying "The closeness, nearness, intimacy to your Creator, God, is what creates and brings close relationship with Him."

When you are far away from a close friend there is no way he or she can say Hey!!! Look there or here; there is no way he can say have you seen so and so? There is no way he can say watch out, there is a pot hole before you. Hey! today you are not looking your best. Hey! Let's go together to lunch or drink tea. Can we travel together to this or that place? Have you seen that person is watching you? Today do not go to that place. The closer you are to a friend the more benefits you get.

Therefore, when we are closer to God the more time, we have to talk to Him also the more time He has to Instruct us. Before I woke up on 16th December, He was giving me a name which I do not think I have at any one time think of, it's a rear name. The Lord said in my heart "Asnath Child" immediately I started praying for that person and child; simple, the Lord had an issue with that name.

"You Do not Know ... " On my morning walk around Muyenga International Hotel men were standing, watching and in my heart I thought they were thinking I was not walking as fast as I could have walked. I received this Word, "You do not know where I have started, What I have gone through to reach here where you have found me." In this world people see others with glitters, and they long to be like them or even better, I have heard stories of Pastors what they have gone through to be what they are, leave alone Presidents. You see entourage, convoys, speed and that prestige that goes with it. Even in Heaven when satan saw the Shekinah Glory of God, the Angels and all the Living Creatures Worshiping God, Lucifer said in Ezekiel "You do not know where they started and what they have gone through."

God has different measures where and how to test His people, some Christians can be tested through lack, others can be tested in the midst of plenty, still a trial is a trial. God uses it to enable you to go to another level so that you do not remain a diaper spiritual baby but you grow from strength to strength. I remember 1986-88 when I was working for the Minister of State for Security. I was under heavy trials, going without food for three to four days with my young children, at times their strength failed and spent some days without going to school because of hunger. This we went through not because there was no way of escape. I had all the channels how to get money and feed my family but because of the fear of the Lord I decided not to Fight for own self.

The Minister of State for Security in Government is highly placed, he had a safe full of all currencies of the world, name it. Due to some pressures and state of his mind at times he used to forget to lock the safe and leave it open. Though I was going through such testing many times I would find myself standing in front of an open safe and all the currencies saying here pick one bundle and your family will quit suffering and I would run close the safe door and keep the key until the Minister returned.

I had an opportunity of making false claims as it was the order of the day for Secretaries to make false claims and get money to feed my family, but because of the faith I had in the Lord I said no, a day is coming when the Lord will up lift me from this situation.

Also, you who has gone through trials suffering through lack or in the midst of plenty do not to ride on a high horse that no one can correct you, cause One can fall from any level, (Rick Joyner, The Call). I heard one Pastor who does not listen to any prophecy or correction of any one in the Church, he says before God talks to anyone about Him, He has to talk to the Pastor first because he says that he is the one who paid the price. *15th December 2011*

Daughter of Judi Zak, Alisa Albers, son Emmanuel, daughter Clare and Gertrude Kabatalemwa

CHAPTER NINETEEN
YOU CAN NEVER SEE THE SUNRISE BY LOOKING TO THE WEST

POSITIONING YOURSELF, You can Never see the Sunrise by Looking to the West. If you position yourself to receive by saying to the Lord "I will take action on what you show me," the Word says that Faith without action is dead. Action springs not from thought, but from readiness for a responsibility. When you get a thought, you get a burden which drives you to action, therefore, position yourself to be ready for responsibility.

There are many people who are excellent reservoirs with storage of learning, academicians, yet never had ideas of changing their environment, e.g. professors, doctors, presidents. "Eyes that Look are many, but those which See are rare.

PEOPLE ARE FLOODED WITH INFORMATION BUT ARE STARVING FOR REVELATIONS.

New ideas die quickly in closed minds, due to lack of interest and aApathy. They say "It's not possible" before they try or "it cannot work, it needs a lot of money to enter into this venture, we need man power which we do not have, etc." Then the enemy comes and deletes or erases the idea out before you take action. Many tries to learn what he already knows. This resembles strongly the Pharisees because they refused to position themselves to receive from Jesus.

Availability is the greatest ability you have, to be in the right place, with the right people, with the right intentions, right ideas and right spirit when an opportunity presents itself. Many people have missed the visitation of the angel of the Lord when He is sent to bring answer to your prayers. A story of a man who missed his opportunity when the angel was sent with an answer to his prayers, due to his familiarity and luck of penitence the angel took his answer and gave it to his neighbor.

Our walk with God begins with the word "Follow" and ends with "Go," e.g. when the Lord called Peter, He said Follow me, and in the Great Commission He says "Go" Preach.

The opportunity God sends won't wake up those who are asleep. Stay on your knees. Pray without ceasing. When God's opportunity comes to know you will be a wake. Kneeling is the proper posture for putting seed into the ground. Christians on their knees see more than the whole world on its tiptoes.

Opportunities can drop on your lap or in your hands if you have your lap or your hands where the opportunity is going to drop. When you do not position yourself to receive, it's like praying for a 200 litre drum of water when you are carrying a plastic mug. You need to enlarge your boundaries, do not ask for so much when your ability is so limited, i.e. you ask God to bless you with a Mercedes Benz when you are still renting in a shanty or ghetto.

We typically see things not as they are or how God sees our potentiality in the spirit, Deuteronomy 1:3-40, 2:14. As we are in our physical environment we should know how we position ourselves, even though we see the evidence of God every where I was helped by Peter's and Robert's circumstances.

AT TIMES OUR MINDS ARE LOCKED UP ON ONE TRACK

At times our minds are locked up on one track, we are looking for red so we ignore or overlook blue. A pastor in the Church was looking for a beautiful girl to marry. The Lord kept showing him a girl with a hunch back, he could not believe it. After a long time he accepted and married the hunchback girl, later when they prayed the hunchback disappeared and out came out the most beautiful girl. A woman with a big head and Gkk with a thyroid gland.

Sometimes, we are thinking of tomorrow and God is saying today or vice versa. We are looking everywhere and the answer is under your nose. When a person is positioned correctly, he is ready to receive all that God has for him.

"When people are free to do as they please they usually imitate each other." Man is the only creation that refuses to be what he is. This has brought disobedience and rebellion because, people have decided to imitate each other. They cannot be innovative, this is when one goes ahead and discover their potential without copying another or doing something or making something without looking at something which existed before.

God made this world, created man and all creation without looking at what there was before. He said "Let there be" and all things came into existence, thus heaven He separated if from the firmament which covered the earth and the water, so there were three different hosts: the sky, the earth and the water body.

When it came to a human being He sat down and said "Let's make man in our own image. God is a spirit, He meant the Spirit, God created the body from the soil as a housing for the Spirit, that's why when man dies the body goes back to the soil and the Spirit goes back to His Creator.

Every animal, fish, bird, reptile has its own kind of food, shelter, communication, reproductive system, movement, protection mechanisms, etc. All creation has obeyed God to how He created them, except man is the only creature that has disobeyed God.

Many have decided to change the Word of God to fulfill their own ego, satisfaction, greed or disobedient and rebellious tendencies.

Let a man marry a man - Homosexuality, gay, bisexual

Let woman marry a woman - Lesbianism

Let man pass law to kill - Abortion

Let man pass law women to sell their bodies - Legal prostitution

Let man sell man for gains - Slavery

Let man murder man to gain riches - Human Sacrifice

Let man change their colour to look more ... - Bleaching

Let man make his own gods - Idoltary

Let man read, write, walk backward (rap) - Quablistic writing (Aliester Crowley)

Man has rebelled against God. He stands and tells God "you are not my God" I just happened from a Big Bang evolution.

Man imitates each other, this is what has brought rebellion in the Church of God. God raises men to serve Him in music, gives them His music to glorify Him, after a few hits, the mixture of the world enters and they start imitating and joining the secular musicians in mass satan worship. When one was asked why he joins in concert with satan worshipping musicians he says; I have to join them in order to win them to the Lord. Darkness does not mix with Light.

They imitate worldly musicians, they go to launch their albums in Hotels to sacrifice God's music on satanic altars with pentagrams and immediately when they do that is when the songs which God had given them to convict sinners to repent become diluted to fit worldly standards to suit and attract more sales. So God's music is played in bars, shrines and on stages of beer brewers and during other commodity promotions. Drunkards and prostitutes sing them without any conviction, in fact they use them to mock Christians. The Godly songs have become more diluted and have lost the meaning for which they were originally intended, to bring sinners to repent.

Whenever we play the song on the crusade drunkards, witches and wizards come out to dance to the tune because the familiar spirit of the devil entered them and they got used to the music like any other worldly ones. They live without Christ. This means the enemy drew out the rocks which were meant to hit and crash the sinner's inner man to bow down to Christ and the essence of the Holy Spirit is no longer there.

The Gospel musicians get the secular world beats so that it makes it easy for drunkards and prostitutes who can dance on those tunes to mock and pervert on them. Those who started dressing humbly, singing on their knees, honouring the Lord now they dress to kill and compete with the secular musicians who are agents of satan.

Pastors have become imitators or copy cats, their messages no longer to appeal to sinners to come to Christ, they are diluted so as not to offend people but condone with sin for fear that if you keep hammering people about sin and walking righteously, they will leave the church, The big sinners are the ones with the big offerings, and they are the elders and deacons in the church. Therefore, pastors are after quantity but not quality sheep who are heaven bound.

Pastors copy each other in passing messages of prosperity, and no longer repent and righteous messages. They tell people the only day of all days God meets His People's Needs is on 31st December, yet God meets the needs of His people daily. By copying each other every pastor has to get a big playground on that day for that day in the year.

Imitating each other has caused them to get involved in the gambling that if one buys many CDs of his message this will let one enter into a raffle to win a car. What the world is doing is business promotion.

Also, they are using all kinds of methods and tricks to attract people to fill up their big cathedrals instead of winning souls for the Lord. Matt 23:13-15, They dictate to people that when they are giving in offering baskets, they should not put in coins but in the Gospel of Mark 12 the poor widow gave a farthing.

One Pastor's wife organized a Conference Seminar using a profane jargon "Girl Power" which came from "Thigh Power" and not even trying to find out the meaning of the Theme. She asked who ever was going to attend the dress code was "Punjab and Shaman" not even trying to find out where these fashions came from and to make matters worse the colours were to be Red and Gold only. Fashion parades or shows are now inside the Churches. After three days or so all women in town are looking for the Dailies to see who was the best dressed woman and the scores at the Christian Conference.

You are fearfully and wonderfully made, Psalm 139:14. Don't copy, be yourself. No one can be exactly like you, even if you are identical twins you differ in the seconds and minutes you take to be born, this makes a difference between you.

"What has made it difficult in this walk is about the ladder, when you are climbing there is a crowd of copied at the bottom or around you, so even if you start or have started well this crowd will try influence you to copy or imitate them." E.g. in Police when recruit takes place by the time one goes through training, the already corrupted copies that you find there will influence you to copy their behavior. You are not created to be all things to all people. When the Lord calls you out many people come out for your help.

You too, as you go God has chosen or given a few people to

help you, not everyone. Special cases of people like Rev Agnes Numer, Sis Judi, Streobel, and John Coast who helped NEEPU. Most flowers have sweet fragrance but we most remember a few, though others also smell good, only one or two are picked and stand out.

CHAPTER TWENTY
PATH OF LEAST RESISTANCE MAKES MEN AND RIVERS CROOKED

FOLLOWING THE PATH OF LEAST RESISTANCE IS WHAT MAKES MEN AND RIVERS CROOKED.

WHAT DOES THIS MEAN? It means that people do not like to work hard, they like to flow the easy way. Copy here and there and make ends meet for survival. They do not like to toil, when they see the mountain or a rock, they dodge it. When they find a big tree they say its big, they cannot remove it first, so they zigzag around it. That's why you find rivers crooked, same as men, they fear responsibility and to work hard, so they start looking for easy come, in the end acquiring bad habits and getting crooked

When you are a copy you adopt yourself to the world, you say that's every one's way, all people are going that direction, I am not special, or I have to follow where everyone is going. Do you really need to follow the crowds even if it is going the wrong way?

The original tries to adapt the world to him. You do not copy the behaviour of this world, but you are a new and different person with a fresh newness in all you do and think. You have your own experiences, rejoicing in hope; patient in tribulation; continuing instant in prayer; Romans 12:2.

It does not take a majority to make a change or transform your surroundings, it is only a few or one determined original with sound cause. Creative ideas do not spring from groups. They spring from individuals. Originals are always hard to find but easy to recognize. God leads every soul in an individual way. There are no precedents: you are the First, 1st you that ever Was!

"There is not enough darkness in the whole world to put out the light that God has put in Me." John 8:12. *25th December 2011*

WE WERE CREATED FOR CONNECTION, GOD DID NOT CREATE us to be a loner, He created us with divine connections. The right friends and associations you meet are not by accident, they were planned by God. These good connections bring out the original in you. God created us to be happy, healthy, peaceful and enjoying life in its fullness. So, these connections are husband, wife, children, friends, Pastors, Sisters and Brothers in the Lord; make these good connections. After you've been with them you find yourself less critical and more full of faith worshipping God and with vision for the future.

It is very important who we closely associate with? Have you ever known a backslider, a friend, sister, brother or Pastor who tried to hang around and pretended to be with you all along yet they was walking on the other side of the road.

The devil doesn't use strangers to deter or stop you. He uses the people who are close to you. Pray for your close associates and the Lord will reveal them to you. The wrong associate brings out the worst in you not the best. When you keep them around then you will find yourself full of doubt, fear, confusion, criticism and judgment that is not of God.

As you grow in the Lord your association changes or will

change. Some of your friends, relatives, Pastors will not want you to prosper spiritually or materially. They will want you to stay where they are because they do not want you to go ahead of them or leave them behind, At least they know that you are not making any progress in the spirit or other areas. Friends who do not help you to climb will want you to crawl or choke your dream. But a good associate will help you to stretch your vision.

Let not anyone talk you out of pursuing a God-given Idea about the Secondary School.

Do not let someone else create your world for you. When they do, they make it too small.

DO NOT LET SOMEONE ELSE CREATE YOUR WORLD FOR YOU. WHEN THEY DO, THEY MAKE IT TOO SMALL.

Who is creating your World? Never receive counsel from unproductive people. Never discuss your problems with someone incapable of contributing to the solution.

Those who never succeed themselves are always first to tell you how to do it and then boast later if you took their advice. (Chris K. of Micro Finance). Not everyone has a right to speak to your life. You will get the worst decisions when you exchange ideas with the wrong people. Do not follow anyone who is going nowhere, especially if they are not following Jesus and the ways of God.

When God gets set to bless you, He brings people into your life. Respect those God has connected to help you.

GOD CARES FOR PEOPLE THROUGH PEOPLE.

E.g. in January 1989 I met Rev. Sis Agnes Numer who was 78 years by then, she introduced me to Sis Judi Zak in May 1993. Judi introduced me to her son–in–law Pastor Tod in April 2005.

We met Bro Robert Streobel in Pastor Tod's Church called Water's Edge Bible Church. Illinois in March 2007, after Moody Radio Talk Show) Pastor Tod introduced me to his dad Pastor Dennis Eenigenburg in May, 2010; Pastor Dennis introduced me to his friend and church member Mr. John Coast in April 2011.

Be careful of the person you stop to inquire for directions along the road of life.

One becomes like those you closely associate with. *31st December 2011*

CHAPTER TWENTY-ONE
THE MOST EXCITING JOURNEY WILL NEVER TAKE PLACE UNLESS YOU TAKE THE FIRST STEP

MESSAGE, Action

A WOMAN IN THE CROWD SHOUTED "GOD BLESS ... AND JESUS replied "Yes, but even more blessed are all who hear the word of God and put it into Practice. Luke 11:27-28. It is more blessed to be a doer of the Word of God than only a hearer.

Dreams do not come true by themselves. The test of a person lies in Action. You know a person by his actions whether hard working or lazy, drunkard, Fighter or adulterer, etc. No person stumbles onto something while sitting down. A fly will be slapped if it does not start working. Sitting still and wishing makes no person great, the Good Lord sends the fish but you have to work out the bait,Anonymous. You learn nothing if you keep talking words without taking action, in the end the words die off. History is made whenever you take action. Proverbs 6:6-8. My favourite proverb says the most exciting journey will never take place unless you take the first step.

You earn respect only by action, inaction earns disrespect.

Some people find life an empty dream because they put nothing into it.

"Thunder is good, thunder is impressive; but it is lighting that does the work."

MARK TWAIN

The test of this teaching is that one student will go saying "It was a good teaching" but another one will take action immediately or later. Make notes and keep revising them and putting them to use. The devil will not stop you to confess faith as long as you do not practice. When praying we must be willing to take action; the answer to your prayers will include action.

There is an old hymn in Church of Uganda which says "Standing on the Promises of God," but when people are singing it they sing when they are sitting down on the promises.

Many people avoid going ahead to discover the secret of success due to the fact that deep down in their hearts they suspect the secret may mean hard work.

Many times, when one sees a big forest standing before you, with big trees, thorns, shrubs, heavy vegetation, and you imagine the snakes, stinging wasps crawling dangerous insects, etc. you loose hope and say it's impossible. But when you gird yourself, get a machete, a leaning stick and begin cutting that forest within no time it will be down. Another Rutooro saying "Someone who does not talk cannot defeat the one who talks."

Our spoken word creates, because we have the creating power in us. Ecclesiastes 3:11.

They defeated the devil and his demons with the Blood of the Lamb and the Word of their testimony. Revelations 12:11.

You may have faith which can remove mountains but if you do not put it into Action it is Dead. *31st December 2011*

LIVING A VICTORIOUS LIFE. WHAT IS VICTORY? VICTORY IS overcoming life's battles. There are many battles we face in life. Some are inherited from ancestral, parental both from paternal and maternal yet others are self caused along the way as you grow through schools and colleges, workmate, associates, friends you acquire, religious beliefs or cults. Also, you can create battles for yourself through wrong marriage yet others can look for you through evil jealous people just because of mere envy.

Victorious life, to be meaningful, has to be experienced Spiritually in Real Life. You may ask that; Can't one be victorious in Real life without being victorious Spiritually? The answer is that there are many people who are prosperous and they think they are victorious because they have all what they want in life. Having material prosperity does not mean victorious living, for at one time or another all material gains will disappear like clouds carried by the wind. "What will benefit you to gain the whole world and lose your own soul?" You can live in the state of your real life in victory with all the glitters, physically fit and fat, dressed in diamonds and pure gold, while your soul is constantly in hunger, lean and on drugs. Then your victory is fake. You need to be well dressed both Spiritually and in Real Life.

Fighting Battles is on Daily Basis. no one can claim to be victorious without going to battle and coming back as a winner. These battles are Spiritual and physical in Real Life. Physical battles are flesh and blood, like boxers in a ring or wrestling; where one says "an eye for an eye, you hurt me, I hurt you," either directly or indirectly. But in Spiritual your battles on your knees praying for your enemies. Vengeance is mine says the Lord, do not Fight for yourself, if one hits your side turn the other side too, e.g. Peter and Robert experiences.

Types of Battles, many battles come directly in physical confrontation, eye for an eye, one will attack you by throwing acid on your face, start a physical Fight, hire gunmen to kill you, come after your wife, child, or property. Other battles come indirectly to hurt your feelings through false accusations, rumours to mud sling you, lies that damage your reputation, satanists engaging you in witchcraft, people ignoring you or giving mean looks, etc.

Spiritual battles wound your soul, where as physical battles maim or cause real physical death. The spiritual man is so sensitive it is easily wounded by mere words, statements, relationships or unforgiveness.

How we get wounded Spiritually if by wrong thoughts, wrong encounters, and wrong company, e.g. this happened to me when I met a person that I knew who was not really close, we used to meet and greet each other. But this time she looked at me and passed by and I did was not bothered at all by her not greeting me, but this started haunting me, causing me to ask myself questions, which started to give me lead accusations like maybe she has been talking to so and so about me, maybe she has been discussing my progress with those who are my rivals etc.

As I went on and on, the Holy Spirit said; by the way, how does this denied greeting bother you. Do you know this will build a negative attitude in your system and wound your spirit? Why do not you change the situation and think something else which will lead you to praise and worship the Lord? Immediately I started a song "We are victorious, brethren do not fear," even though there are trials coming along, Jesus knows us and lets stand as Victors. That was the end of the matter, I got this message.

In the physical one may get a pimple, when you keep

scratching it, at times it can get septic and result into a wound, but if you leave it alone it will ripe by itself and heal on its own. Thus some times when a situation happens, just give it time it will work out itself and heal on its own. People who live in villages go to work in gardens, there are types of thorns, when it gets into your skin, just give it time, the skin will reject it and will come out by itself, but when you continue bothering it, if it decides to be stubborn it will get contagious and result in a big boil. Therefore, in life there are some times small issues we keep prodding they become septic and result into big issues, when they are to be given time in order to solve themselves..

How do you get defeated through thoughts? Many people have been defeated in the area of thoughts when they get carried away and do not ask the Holy Spirit "What can I do in a situation which is tense like this?" There are times weird thoughts about someone you meet, who used to greet you, now he ignores you, or gives you a mean look or if you fell apart or have fallen apart with your dad, mom, child, husband, wife, workmate, friend or relative. The negative thoughts will flood your mind, you start building fences, digging trenches, dumping garbage all around you and forget that you are also blocking yourself; when you want to come out you will have no way of escape and your wound deepens.

How do we get over or deter Spiritual wounds? When wild thoughts come along the way to block you from your vision, do not give them a breeding ground, cut them off and create a positive attitude. Think of something creditable, some good things which God has done for you of recent or other times.

When you are in a fix of a situation and having differences with the beloved ones, always leave a way of escape by not going too far to block yourself with a lot of statements of accusing, self defense or incriminating, do not say much. Keep a distance and avoid places where you can easily bump into each other to cause confrontation, keep away from places which can bring back bad memories unless if it is for a testimony to give God the Glory. This depends on the seriousness of the issue.

Spiritual Victory and Real-Life Victory works out, all is well with your soul when it is dressed in the Garment of Salvation and a Robe of Righteousness. *12th January 2012*

CHAPTER TWENTY-TWO
SIX BARREN WOMEN

MESSAGE, Seeking God, And Joash did that which was right in the sight of the LORD all the days of Jehoiada the priest, 2 Chronicles 24:1-7.

As we were coming from the village I felt that I had to buy a big chicken before I began my 10 days fast on water and honey. We bought it near Nabingoora, when we reached home Tom prepared it and we ate it for two days on 30th and 31st January. I am seeking to draw close to the Lord in intimacy and to give all my effort to please the Lord. All for God and His Glory as long as I live.

He gives strength to the weary and to him who lacks might He increases power. Though youth grow weary and tired and vigorous young men stumble badly. Yet those who wait upon the Lord will gain new strength; they will mount up with wings like eagles. They will run and not get tired. They will walk and not become weary. Isaiah 40:29-31.

To seek the Lord to know His Will concerning my children what went wrong as I am the one to support them instead of them supporting me and the School projects in the village.

Clare was struggling working without any salary, struggling

with CIS which yields only for high rents for both of us working without salaries.

Robert who got frustrated and disgusted left without a word now, gone 10 years with me not seeing him or hearing from him.

Peter had a sensible job, except on a construction site with a pay from hand to mouth.

Emma had applied for a genuine visa four times to study with a Scholarship granted by Liberty University. He was denied.

Next, on 24th January 2012 all recommendation to travel on my behalf to meet and do a follow-up on sponsorship, this visa was also denied.

Rent I put before the Lord the burden of renting which has become so much on me, I need the Lord's hand to lift this burden.

On the evening 1st February 2012 a letter from the landlord was brought to me Increasing my rent from 700,000/= - 8500,000/=.

On 3rd Sunday Clare came to spend a day with me and she was almost in tears telling me that she was so perturbed. She was kind of saying that she was about going to cohabit with ... I was so taken up. I had a long sharing with her about long suffering and Six Barren Women in the Bible and when they waited the Lord gave them the desires of their heart. *1st February 2012*

SIX BARREN WOMEN, GOD USED BARREN WOMEN TO GIVE birth to Mighty Men and Over-comers in God's Service. Sarah, was a wife of Abraham. A child was promised to Abraham in his youth so they prayed until they reached a very old age and had even lost hope, then Sarah gave birth to Isaac, a Patriarch, Gen. 15:4, and chapters 17-21.

Rebecca, even after many years of marriage, she had no children, she was a barren. Isaac pleaded with Jehovah to give

Rebecca a child, then at last she became pregnant and gave birth to twin brothers, Esau and Jacob. Jacob was the father to 12 tribes of Israel. Gen. 25:21.

Rachel, was a wife of Jacob and she was a barren. Gen. 30:22.. Then God remembered Rachel's plight and answered her prayers by giving her a child she named Joseph. Joseph was the one who was sold to Egypt by his brothers and caused the Israelites to go to Egypt as God promised Abraham in Gen. 15:13 and Ex. 12:40.

Manoah's wife Manoah and his wife lived in the city of Zorah she had no children but the angel said to her "Even though you have been barren for so long, you will conceive and have a son," Samson was their son and God used him to punish the Philistines. Judges 13.

Hannah was a wife of Elkanah and although he loved Hannah very much ... the Lord had sealed her womb; she had no children to give presents to. ... The Lord remembered Hannah's petition in the process of time a baby boy was born to her she named Samuel who became a great Judge for Israel. 1 Samuel 1:1-20.

Elizabeth was a wife of Zacharias and they had no children, for Elizabeth was a barren, and now both they were very old. But an angel Lord said, "Do not be afraid, Zacharias! For I have come to tell you that God has heard your prayer, and your wife Elizabeth will bear you a son! And you are to name him John. John was the forerunner of our Lord Jesus Christ. Luke 1:7-60.

God cannot use a person until He hurts him most, Not because He hates you but there is need to prepare you for a great testimony. Everybody God uses has a testimony bearing witness whether of long-suffering, shame or another. Sarah's testimony was of bearing the shame of having no child up to 90 years for Hagar. Rebbeca's testimony was two nations in her womb and a scheme for Jacob to cheat his brother. Rachel's testimony was the desperation for a child and how she abused her servant. Manoah's wife's testimony was the visitation of the angel from God. Hannah's testimony was the taunting of her co-wife Peninnah and accusations of being drunk. Elizabeth's testimony was bearing the shame to the old age without a child. 2nd February 2012

GOD CHOSE SAUL AS A KING FOR ISRAEL AFTER THE Israelites refused God to be their King. This grieved Samuel so much until God told him that do not you worry, I chose them a King it's me they have rejected to be their King, 1 Samuel 9.

Human beings goes with 4 senses; see, touch, taste and hear. The Israelites wanted to have a human king whom they could see, touch, hear, and talk to like other nations around them, yet God was doing everything they needed and wanted, even making them win all their battles. 3rd February 2012

WHEN GOD'S FAVOUR IS UPON YOU, IT CAN CAUSE KINGS TO turn all their hearts, heads and riches towards you. Ezra 6, 7. Our God Fights our battles. He is a warrior and Jehovah is His name. Exodus 15:3.

During the reign of Artaxerxes, the enemies of the Jews; Bishlam, Mithredath and Tabeel and their associates wrote letters to him in Aramaic language accusing the Jews for building the Temple and these letters were translated to him, this included the Governor Rehun, Shimshai, a scribe-Secretary, several judges and other local leaders of the Persians and Babylonians men of Erech and Susa and men from other nations. Ezra 4.

King Cyrus father of Darius, the father of Ar-ta-xerxes Kings of Persia King Darius himself ordered the search of the Records concerning the Temple of God in Jerusalem and they were found in the palace in Achmetha.

After the death of king Darius, his son king Cyrus continued with what his father had started and issued a decree that a Temple of God in Jerusalem should be built and gave strong instructions: "Do not disturb the construction of the Temple ..." Ezra 6:1-6.

I am confused here, about the letter's authority and Darius authority ...

Darius issued a decree that those heathen pay the full construction costs without delay and also gave priests in Jerusalem young bulls, ram and lambs for burnt offerings to the God of heaven. He gave them wheat, wine, salt, and olive oil each day without fail. Then they were able to offer acceptable sacrifices to the God of heaven and to pray for him and his sons.

Anyone who attempted to change the message in any way shall have Darius issued a decree that, The God who has chosen the city of Jerusalem will destroy any king or any nation that alters this commandment and destroys this Temple. I, Darius, have issued this decree, let it be obeyed with all diligence. Ezra 6:12.

When you are in God's favour even those who oppose you will turn to you and seek refuge, and worship the same God you worship and eat from your table.

And some of the heathen people who had been relocated in Judah turned from their immoral customs and joined the Israelis in worshiping the Lord God. They along with the entire Jewish nation, ate the Passover feast.

God's favour was found when, Artaxerxes decreed that any Jew in his realm including priests and Levites may return to Jerusalem with Ezra. The King and his Council of Seven instructed Ezra to take a copy of God's laws to Judah and Jerusalem and send back the report. The King and his Council of Seven commissioned Ezra to take with him silver and gold as an offering to the God of Israel. If you run short of money for the construction of the Temple or for any similar needs you may requisition funds from the Royal Treasury, Ezra 6.

Because of the favour, fear and respect for God in you, people will give all they have to gain your favour.

King Artaxerxes gave another decree to all the treasurers in the provinces west of the Euphrates River saying ou are to give Ezra whatever *he requests of you* for ... a*n*d *w*hatever *else the* G*o*d *of H*ea*v*en demands for His Temple; for why should we risk God's wrath against the king and his sons? I also decree that no priest, Levite choir member, gate keeper, Temple attendant or other worker in the Temple shall be required to pay taxes of any kind!!!

Kings and rulers will entrust your wisdom and give you power to select and appoint your own staff and to punish whoever does not obey.

And you Ezra, are to use the wisdom God has given you to select and appoint judges and other officials to govern all the people west of Euphrates River, that is within the kingdom of Babylon. If they are not familiar with the laws of your God you are to teach them. Anyone refusing to obey the laws of your God and the Law of the king shall be punished immediately by death, banishment, confiscation of goods or imprisonment. Ezra 7. *4th February 2012*

CHAPTER TWENTY-THREE
ENVY PROVIDES THE MUD AND FAILURE THROWN AT SUCCESS

"When others throw bricks at you, turn them into stepping-stones."

YOU'RE BORN AN ORIGINAL DO NOT DIE A COPY BY JOHN MASON.

ALL GREAT IDEAS CREATE CONFLICT, misunderstanding, headaches and clashes. In other words, your destiny creates challenges and criticism in some people. When you have great ideas, some people will say "That is impossible, you are wasting time, this cannot work here, many people have tried but have failed. You have money to waste, it will not last." As the gossips goes on these days saying she gets money from under water, she cuts people's heads that is where she gets that kind of money. But few others will say you have a good project, we need to support it, nothing good has ever happened to this place like this one.

Let our response to critics be what the Bible says: We are perplexed, but not in despair, persecuted, but not forsaken, cast down, but not destroyed, 2 Corinthians 4:8-9. When the devil's agents fail to stop you by mud slinging you, damaging your reputation and see you have kept a deaf ear through desperation they will turn to witchcraft and other satanic activities.

But criticism of the children of God is the language of the devil to discourage us. The Bible says the devil is the accuser of the brethren. Criticism is always a part of supernatural promotions, When your head sticks up above the crowd, expect more criticism than buffets. satan always attacks those who can hurt him the most.

God works from the inside out, the devil tried to work from the outside in, to hurt your feelings by throwing words that can hurt you, e.g. one gentle man was so much disturbed by Nyamabuga Primary School Project that he sat among people and told them that he almost got her, when she was going to cut the heads off people, but she escaped from me near River Sogahi. One member cautioned him and said you do you know if you say things without proof and she gets to know what you are saying and take you to court you can pay heavily. You need to withdraw that statement.

Whoever criticizes others to you will criticize about you to others also, take note. You can always tell failures by the way they criticize the success of others. Let me tell you if there were no hard workers around the critics would soon be out of business. We have a man who wakes up early in the morning and goes to the trading centre by 6.00am and starts knocking on doors waking people so that he can enter and start criticizing whatever is going on around.

Envy provides the mud and failure thrown at success. Critics that throw mud are simultaneously losing ground and small minds are the first to condemn great ideas.

(Owihali akoma ebisabu ahereza byaleema, byaleema ahungurra ogu e'wemirimo ye yarabiremu. Kandi abo abagaya nibahungura ebisaabu, baikara nibagaruka enyuma, n'obwongo bwabo obutaito bucwera omusango entekereza eyamagezi). If people talk negatively about you, ignore them and keep working in the long run no one will believe them. Fear of criticism is a hindrance to progress of achieving your goal, if you are afraid of criticism you will die doing nothing.

A successful man is the one who can lay a firm foundation with the mud which is turned into bricks that others throw at Him. 5th February 2012

CHAPTER TWENTY-FOUR
CAN AN EXTENSION
FUNCTION WITHOUT BEING
PLUGGED IN?

I GOT these very important High Points which touched my heart.

Lawrence of Arabia, before he was called Thomas Edward, was born 16th August 1888. He was engaged in desert raids with his Arab friends in World War I. He wrote Adventures in The Seven Pillars of Wisdom. After the war he formed close friendships with many sheiks of Arabia. After the war he brought some of them back to England to show his appreciation for their support against the Turkish they conquered. He took the sheiks to visit the Joint House of Commons and Parliament where they had audience with the queen. On the last day of their visit Lawrence offered them anything they wanted to take back with them to their desert homes. The sheiks led him up into the hotel room in to the bathroom and pointed to the faucets in the bath tab. They wanted these to provide them with running water in the desert. Food for the thought, really, can a faucet provide water without a plumbing process?

In the year 1847 a doctor from Edinburg England named Sir James Simpson, discovered that chloroform could be used as an anesthesia to render people insensible of pain during surgery making it possible for people to go through the most dangerous operations without fear of suffering. This was a most significant discovery for modern medicine. Some years later, while lecturing at the University of Edinburg a student asked "What do you consider to be the most valuable discovery of your life time?" Instead of referring to chloroform, Dr. Simpson said "My most valuable discovery was when I discovered myself a sinner and that Jesus Christ was my Saviour." *7th February 2012*

READ MESSAGES FROM THE IPAD ABOUT GOD'S TRUE GRACE vs False Grace. *8th February 2012*

THE LORD WAS GIVING ME INSTRUCTIONS FROM Deuteronomy 26. Read it all. *9th February 2012*

FINAL DAY OF TEN DAYS OF SEEKING THE LORD, I STARTED with my salvation came from the Lord because in the line of my father my mother there was no trace of salvation, all people perished. But the Lord has saved me by the Grace to cause many to find salvation in order to pay back for all those souls of my ancestors who could not make it to the Lord.

On 9th February the Lord gave me the grace to go through many of my diaries from 1987 and I came across the fact that most of the petitions I made at the beginning of my ten day journey seeking the Lord were earlier petitioned. However, on this day, I put it before the Lord that the Intimacy, closeness and close relationship with the Lord was answered in all what I was petitioning: Intimacy, when you are in the Lord and the Lord is in you, ask for whatever you want and it shall be given to you: spiritual, or physical, beauty is automatic as Moses the patriarch went to Mt. Sinai to collect the 10 commandments, when he returned his face was shining and his face shined so as the people could not see him directly, so he had to cover his face. After some time, the light started to fade away. However, for now, because of the Blood of Jesus, when we choose to be in close relationship with Him, we do not wane away, we stay young and shining.

When you are in a high secret place with the Lord your children and beloved ones are covered with salvation and righteousness that will be provided as well as security. Homes will be given, isn't the Lord the giver of all good gifts?

Today Lord I receive all those petitions I made for your service as my slogan goes:

Here I am for your Take, for your Keep, and for your Use, Holy Spirit Lead, Guide and Direct me in all your righteousness. Amen. Quote of Gertrude K.

Lord as you revealed to me on 2nd February 2012 that Barren Women gave birth to Great men for your Kingdom Services; Sarah, Rebecca, Rachel, Hannah, Manoah's wife and Elizabeth. So, let me today, after all what I went through since when I became Born Again, May I be born to you a New Kabatalemwa Gertrude into your Great Service too?

When I am born to you for your Take, for your Keep and for your Use, and the Holy Spirit Leading, Guiding and Directing me, let me be under your Garment of Humility. That I will not raise my head but keep lifting your Name. Deut.7, Read it all again the Lord giving me Instructions. *10th February 2012*

Message, Abide in me, ... I am the vine, John 15:4-5, Jeremiah 17:9, Psalms 1, 2, 3

Plugging, after receiving a team from Louisiana led by Pastor Dennis with Bro John Coast, Bro Kit, Bro Bret, Bro Don and Bro Jon. On their way to the hotel the van stuck on the way at Rwibale, I hired a taxi to collect them, we arrived at Fort Motel at 11.00pm very tired.

Early in the morning of 20th, I received in my spirit that we have to keep plugged in, in order to function in the Spirit of the Lord. A question was paused before me that: "Can an extension function without being plugged in the socket?"

The answer: Until the appliance is plugged in or a switch turned on that is when you receive the power. You do not see the power in the wall but it is there because it is a system which was wired into the walls when they were being built. It is you to tap on that power. Other houses or property the pipes were layed in the walls but power is not yet there, others the pipes and wires were all laid there but power was or is not yet taped there, so they remain in darkness. The story of Lawrence of Arabia on 7th February 2012 and the Faucet.

Your mobile phone is like a box if it not connected to host until you buy the line and you are connected it will not call any one. When you are spiritually plugged in and connected, that is how you get intimacy with your Creator, that is how you cultivate or activate that relationship. When you keep plugged in and connected you will enjoy the Intimacy, Relationship, Trust, Confidence, and Presence of the Creator. *19th February 2012*

The Present Moral and Ethical failure, in these last days moral and ethics of Christians have derailed due to self satisfaction of the worldly gains. Pastors are faced with rivalry and competition, pride, prosperity doctrines, and wrong advice. Gospel Music Artists seem to compete with rivalry, they compromise, and have become copy cats.

Preachers and Evangelists are in disobedience abandoning their callings.

Believers have become dependent on their Pastors, and cannot scratch for themselves, some involved with witchcraft.

27th February 2012

CHAPTER TWENTY-FIVE
GRAB OUR BRETHREN BACK

ZIKLAG MESSAGE, after Sunday Service with Sommer and Rebbecca we went to visit Loy and Richard Bangirana and share. Bro Bangirana told me twice he had visions and a dream about me of the enemy cutting the ankles of my legs. I went back home and cried to the Lord to show me where I was going wrong. Before morning the Lord revealed it to me that I was having a sin of Judgment of brothers. I cried so much and repented, this was not the first time, I had had it some time back and I repented then forgot and started again. The Lord reminded me when Twesige came and gave me the message that "Why the Lord loves me is because I know how to look out for myself" Kweserra.

On this point I was this time dead serious in repentance and promised to start praying for the Pastors and the Born-Again Church in Uganda and other parts of the world. The sin of judging was eating me up and there the enemy was trying to put me in a position "Self-righteousness." As there are so many things going on in the Born-Again Churches, I was being eaten up by pointing fingers, putting myself in the place of a Judge.

At this time I remembered the Ziklag message three days

later, when David and his men arrived home at their city of Ziklag, they found that the Amalekites had raided the city and burned it to the ground, carrying off all women and children. As David and his men looked at the ruins and realized what had happened to their families, they wept until they could weep no more. Then he said to Abiathar the priest, "Bring me the ephod" so Abiathar brought it and David asked the Lord, "Shall I chase them? Will I catch them?" And the Lord told him, "Yes, go after them, you will recover everything that was taken from you!"

Brethren we need to chase the Amalekites who have raided and burnt our city to the ground and carried off all our families andbelongings. We ask the Lord "Shall I chase them? Will I catch those demons?" The Lord, our God, is the God of the past, present and future, the Lord is holding those Amalekites (demons) in a drunken stupor. They are spread out across the fields, eating and drinking and dancing with joy because of the loot they have taken from the brethren.

The Lord knew that David and his men would not be put to shame, so He held those Amalekites there and did not allow them to do any harm to wives and children of His people. So David and his men rushed in among them and slaughtered them all that night and the entire next day until evening. No one escaped. 1 Samuel 30.

You also, you are crying, grumbling the Lord your God is watching over your lost child, husband, father, or mother pleading that no harm should come to him or her, because He cares. My son Peter, for 22 years, no harm came to him in West Africa. One day he asked me where he drew all the strength, I laughed because he said then he was still in captivity where he was kidnapped.

That one day he had a motor bike accident and his body was mangled, was hospitalized, and within three days he was out, healed and very strong as if nothing had happened. That his body heals quickly by itself. I told him that I had prayed to the Lord that he will not come back home maimed, that he will return to me whole, indeed God heard my prayers.

On 22nd December 2011 with his Brother Emma had a very bad accident on a Diggi Motorcycle. The Lord had told me a week before of the accident and I prayed no one had a serious injury. The Lord knows the past, present and future and takes care of them without your knowledge, because you are His beloved. When the Lord knew what David was going to do to the house of Nabal He sent Abigail to run and meet David, she took provision to abate David's anger where he had promised to kill everyone in Nabal's household. David when he heard that Nabal was dead he said; Praise the Lord God has paid back Nabal and kept me from doing it myself. 1 Samuel 25:19-39.

Last but not least at this point the Lord reminded me of Bro Rick Joyner's Book "The Final Quest." That when Christian brethren were being herded like prisoners by the enemy, fellow Christians followed behind them throwing poisonous arrows and piercing them with swords wounding them the more, instead of bandaging their wounds they were tearing away the bandages and leaving them with open wounds and that some fellow Christians were hurting them more than the enemy.

Therefore, if the Amalekites have carried our brothers away we should go after them and grab our brethren back, by shooting arrows of intercession prayers which will bring them back to their senses. *4th March 2012*

FIRST DAY IN BUNGA HOUSE, I OPENED, AS USUAL, THE scriptures to the spot where it was Joshua 1 about God's charge to

Joshua. This was my 1st day in the house of Bunga. I had arrived with Sommer and Rebbecca from the village on the eve of 6th March, I took time to anoint and pray for the house. On the eve of 7th, Sommer left for Home. *7th March 2012*

CHAPTER TWENTY-SIX
GOD MAKES A PODIUM FOR HIS PEOPLE

MESSAGE, Joshua assumes command, Joshua 1:10-18. Rahab sheltered the spies who were sent to spy out Jericho, Joshua 2.

What I learnt is that the Israelites said; just as we obeyed Moses - Leader in all things, so we will ... only may the Lord Your God be with you as He was with Moses. They disowned God as their God and called Him a God of Joshua and Moses. Instead of saying "May the Lord "Our" God be with "Us." Rahab said for we have heard how the Lord dried up the waters of the Red Sea before you when you came out of Egypt and what you did to the five kings of the Amorites beyond the Jordan, also Sihon and Og you utterly destroyed. Look the heathen far from, as far as Jericho, could still remember what God did after 78 years when the Israelites were in the wilderness, but the Israelites could not remember even for a short time when Moses went to Mt. Sinai to get the Ten Commandments, they had forgotten what God had done for them with the Red Sea. Rahab, the prostitute, honoured and recognized the Sovereignty of the Lord and said the Lord your God, He is God in Heaven above and on earth. Joshua 1, 2.
8th March 2012

MESSAGE, GOD MAKES A PODIUM FOR HIS PEOPLE,

Pharaoh sent and called for Joseph and they hurriedly brought him out of the dungeon, and when he had shaved and changed his clothes ... Pharaoh said to Joseph, I have had a dream, but no one can interpret it, and I have heard, it said about you, that when you hear a dream you can interpret it. Joseph then answered Pharaoh, saying It is not in me, God will give Pharaoh a favourable answer ... then Joseph interprets the dream for Pharaoh. Joseph is made a ruler of Egypt. Pharaoh said to his servants, "can we find a man like this in whom is a divine spirit?" Genesis 41:14-32.

So, Pharaoh said to Joseph, since God has informed you of all this, there is no one so discerning and wise as you are. You shall be over my house, and according to your command all of my people shall do homage, only in the throne I will be greater than you. Then Pharaoh, took off his signet ring from his hand, and put it on Joseph's hand, and clothed him in garments of fine linen and put the gold necklace around his neck.

God is making a podium for you where you have no guess or dream about. Joseph was there in prison he had lost hope, being in a foreign land, taken as a slave, thrown in prison for no good reason, who could have pleaded for him? Even when he interpreted the dreams of the two king's officials, t and one who was restored to position, Joseph pleaded with him that please when you go back remember to put a good word for me before the king that I was thrown in prison maliciously. Still the official forgot. When people are out of trouble they forget, but when they need your help the grass will never grow at your door step.

On the other hand, we cannot blame the man, he had no suitable moment to mention Joseph to Pharaoh until God brought in the right occasion by giving Pharaoh a dream so complicated dream which no one could interpret to him. This made the official to remember Joseph because the time had come for God to make a Podium for Joseph. Joseph ruled the whole of Egypt because God had to fulfill the Word He gave to Abraham in Genesis. Now Joseph was thirty years old when he stood before Pharaoh, king of Egypt. Joseph bought all the land of Egypt for Pharaoh, for every Egyptian sold his field, because a famine was severe upon them. Thus, the land of became Pharaohs.

Therefore, there is a famine of the Word of God in the land and our Lord who is looking for a person who is going to bring His people out of a famine, not of food, but a famine of the Word of God. He is looking for a Joseph to make a Podium for him in order to purchase the hearts of Catholics, Protestants, Muslims, Seven Adventists, etc. The famine has covered the whole earth and the Lord is looking around and asking whom can He send.

Joseph made it a statute concerning the land of Egypt valid to this day that Pharaoh owns a fifth of the land of Egypt because all those people came and sold their land to Joseph in order to get food and not starve.

However, even now people are starving for the true Word of God and are ready to sell everything, even their souls, in order to get food for their souls. Many people are already selling their souls to the devil through his deception when he takes them to the under world, under water for initiation that he is going to give them eternal rest lie.

Purify yourself and the Lord is going to make a podium for you to purchase souls for Him of those who are almost to perishing in Famine of the Word of God. *23rd March 2012*

CHAPTER TWENTY-SEVEN
DO YOU NOT FEAR THE LORD?

THE HOLY SPIRIT led me to this message: Do you Not Fear the Lord?

NOW HEAR THIS, O FOOLISH AND SENSELESS PEOPLE WHO have eyes but do not see, who have ears but do not hear. Do you not fear me, declares the Lord? Do you not tremble in my Presence? I have placed the sand as a boundary for the sea, An eternal decree, so it cannot cross over It ...

This should tell us the greatness of the Lord our God. How big is a speck or grain of a single bit of sand? The Lord aligned all the sand together and made them a boundary for the mighty waves of the seas and oceans. Who can stop a mighty wave when it comes tossing, roaring and standing like a giant mountain? Only the little grains of sand stop it because the Lord said inThus far you shall come, but no farther. And here shall your proud waves stop, Job 38:11.

The enemy has come against you like a flood, he comes roaring and tossing to crash you.

You look at yourself, so small like a grain of the sand, but there is One who is greater than the mighty giant waves, storm, tornado, like a tsunami in you, who will say so far and no farther, and all that flood will roll back in shame.

The queen of evil, they call her a queen of heaven, she is dressed in a black robe with a hood holding an evil baby and a serpent entangled on her ankle as in the movie of the Passion of Christ. She coming after everybody on the earth to attack them! Now her green fields are in the Born Again Churches and her mighty, proud waves are coming like a great mountain to sweep the church from the shore and take it back with her into the deep sea giving them the treasures of the Titanic and other ship liners which sank with a mighty crowd of kings and leaders of all nations, from all colours, languages, scholars, wise men and big names with invited commas and brackets the monetary gurus.

The queen of evil and her cohorts see the Children of God who testify and have the testimony of Christ the Lord; they laugh, belittle, despise and persecute them with their proud waves. They see just a grain or speck of sand, very weak, then sends waves come over and wash them off shore.

But the Word of God lives forever it cannot change, it remains the same now and forever.

Thus far you shall come, but no farther, Job 38:11. And here shall your Proud waves stop. Christians are winners, even if they kill us we germinate out of one killed, 1000 are more are saved because of the Blood of Jesus.

My first time I saw the roaring ocean I was in Long Island, New York in 1990 when my friends took me to the beach for the first time. When I saw the big waves coming, I thought we were all going to be washed into the ocean but my friends assured me that the waves were going to roll back as they came in but I was still almost screaming my heart out.

God can put to a stop any huge object with a teeny weeny thing like an anchor on a ship, my how it stops a big vessel carrying 6,000-8,000 people plus cargo. Therefore, we should fear and Worship such a God who stops roaring gigantic sea waves with a grain of sand. God has taken wondrous Blessings.

The Lord continues to lament; but my people have rebellious hearts, they have turned against me and gone off into idolatry. Though I am the one who gives them rain each year in spring and fall and sends the harvest times, yet they have no respect or fear for me. And so I have taken way these wondrous blessings from them. Jeremiah 5:24-25. This sin has robbed them of all of these good things.

Yes, the Lord is right, we are living in the days of rebellion, where the world is moving forward at a supersonic speed with new technology and nearly everything is computerized so without using people you pay salaries, pay water, pay electricity, receive money, open gates, drive cars, pilot planes, guide Ocean Liners to mention but a few. People are not stopping to look back and think "History repeats itself!" As it was in the days of Noah, Lot, and Nimrod of the Tower of Babel who was killed by Shem the son of Noah. So, who knows what kind of tsunami is coming next time.

The Lord said that those people did all that rebelliousness He is the one who gives them rain each year in spring and fall and sends the harvest times, yet they have no respect or fear for Him!!!

The Lord swears that He has taken away those wondrous blessings from them. Rain blessing may mean good health, many people you see them walking but when they go into their homes in their bedroom they are groaning, thoughts accumulating, wondering that maybe this could be my last year on the earth, where do I leave all my riches I have accumulated?

There is a Moslem rich man I know in town who has a couple of wives, built a mansion for each on a hill, went to another big hill and built himself a dream house overlooking the city.

To my surprise, one day I met him in one of the big towns driving a very expensive vehicle but failed to recognize him. He looked like a secondary boy in a short sleeved shirt with a cap close to his nose to avoid to be recognized, his face and arms were as if he had scabies, I tried to recognize him but could not, until when he was gone, I said to myself I think this could have been, who? In the hay days of AIDS in Uganda he used to drink from a mug with an inscription on it: "The sexiest man in the City," boasting to his wife, children and people in the house.

You have no respect or fear for the Lord; He says He has taken away wondrous blessings from you which may mean having no job, you have completed your studies, you have a degree, after the degree you went for Masters but now its 2, 3, 4 or 5 years with no job for you. You dress up and go to the city, people admire how smart you are, but inside you are almost bursting to tears and planning suicide in the next few moments.

You have no respect or fear for the Lord, you cheat on your husband, your wife, you lie, you go to visit witchdoctors, you fornicate and the Lord has taken away those wondrous blessings of joy in your marriage. Your marriage is a storm in the tea cup. One morning an engineer came to see me in my office and we were discussing something important.

When we finished I said good day then he busted in tears and I got scared wondering whether I had said something which caused him to sob. I started comforting him when he said I am coming from court for a divorce, my wife has taken my children away to her Southern Africa home and she has fallen in love with a white man. After comforting him I asked him; You say you are a Born Again Pastor and he said yes. I told him "You have a big problem! Go and try to find yourself!!!"

You plant much but harvest little, you have scarcely enough to eat or drink, and not enough clothes to keep you warm. Your income disappears, as though you were putting it into pockets filled with holes. Haggai 1:6.

You have no respect or fear of the Lord. The Lord has taken away those wondrous blessing from you. You eat but you do not get satisfied, you drink your thirst is not quenched, you get money it disappears, the Lord has filled your pockets with holes. The day you get your salary is when you are called by your mother who was bitten by a dog, thieves attacked your mother and almost killed her or your child has been knocked by a boda boda taxi . The day you receive money that is when you meet conmen and they tell you they have magic that can multiply what you have a 100 fold and so you lose all what you were paid.

You have no respect or fear of the Lord. The Lord has taken way those wondrous blessings from you. He has given you a beautiful voice to preach the Gospel through singing, to counsel, uplift, and comfort those who are in despair and gladden the heart of His people, but you have started to call the songs. He gave you your songs and you started trading yours with them. You have become a copy due to the fact that … . No wonder, Bro John Mason said "You are born an original, do not die a copy."

The Lord said lastly; This sin has robbed them all of these things. Jeremiah 5:25.

Shouldn't I punish a Nation like this? The Lord God asks; shouldn't I punish Israel, a Nation like this? These people of the nation the Lord wants to punish are the: foolish, senseless who have eyes that do not see, have ears that do not listen, have no respect at all for Him, they do not tremble in His presence, do not fear or worship Him and they have rebellious hearts.

Among my people are wicked men who lurk for victims like a hunter hiding in a blind darkness. They set their traps for men like a coop full of chickens their homes are full of evil plots nd the results Now they are great and rich, well fed and well groomed, and there is no limit to their wicked deeds. They refuse justice to orphans and the rights of the poor. Jeremiah 5:26-29.

The Lord has sworn to punish the nation of people who are hiding among the believers.

"Praise the Lord" has become like a club or society salutation. They say "Whoever is not saved now, it's a shame." So, "Praise the Lord" for the Savedees has become a slogan.

Many wicked men and women have hidden behind the curtain of Born Again Savedees Churches; they set their traps to catch true seekers of God and they have joined Church for business gains.

Some go underworld to fetch fake power to perform miracles to deceive the people of God that they are working under the Power of the Holy Spirit. They make people drink dirt water calling it Holy Water, they take advantage of widows, or sodomize orphans who come desperately seeking after God. Many good people have fallen in wrong hands of wicked men who hide in Churches using the names of pastor, elder, deacon, etc. They manipulate people to give in money, create occasions and programmes in order to keep the continuation of flowing money and in order to build big cathedrals. The Lord has told me they are a Coop full of chickens where they hatch evil plots.

And the results are now they are great and rich and go to buy 500m vehicles as if the gospel has reached every corner of the world according to the Lord's Command that is: Go and Preach the Gospel ... They go pushing and scratching their fat bellies, wearing trousers with suspenders and have no limit to their deeds. On two occasions I met one popular pastor and I tried to share about a hot issue concerning the Church, but he looked at me with a look like "what's wrong with you?" That is not what we are about and paid no attention at all. Some men pastors go with lip shiners to shine their lips in public.

Our Church leaders are copy cats. Do not copy the behaviours of this world, but be a new and different person with fresh newness in all you do and think. This will be because when you are climbing the ladder of success you get through the crowd of copies at the bottom. When you listen are they praying changing voices to sound like pastor so and so?

I have a little boy in our Village Church very innocent and committed to the ways of God. When he started to pray, he started cracking his voice to sound like the pastor, how he cracks his voice, I just wondered, later I called him and told him "Be yourself, do not copy anybody or how they pray, God wants to listen to you in your child's voice, not in some pastor's voice.

Some Gospel Music artists after when the Lord called them they started miming the secular world artists. Dressing to kill on stage competing with the worldly artist, one Christian lady went to launch her song, she was dressed in 1m/ dress she was all glitters like lady gaga in a meat dress on her 26th birthday. The Lord's singers use same venues where Worldly singers go for Pam Award Hotel Halls with Pentagrams designed for devil worship and sacrifice their voices there.

Take notice now most Gospel singers who have gone the way of the world no longer sing songs to exalt God but to look for songs to praise people, composed songs to entertain crowds on introduction functions, storytelling of girls. It is like Nigerian movies where by they play all witchcrafts, violence, sex and immorality for 40 minutes and then 5 minutes they bring in church. What about if someone was sitting for 40 minutes and decided to leave before the 5 minute part comes in, what picture will he go with

People do not play with the queen of evil sitting in heaven not sleeping and using every venue to hook children of God.

I am not saying all this that I try to judge and despise the Church leaders, it is not all of them but those who have left the ancient ways and have become copies. Trace the part where you lost your way and come back.

And with all this the Lord is asking Should I sit back and act as though nothing is going on? Shouldn't I punish a Nation such as this? Jeremiah 5:19-31.

A horrible thing has happened in this land!!! The Lord is saying; "A horrible thing has happened in this Land, the priests are ruled by false prophets and my people like it so!" But your doom is certain. This is really horrible, because priests have never had time to go and seek the Lord and they say there is no power in our churches, they go to seek false power from false prophets and witch doctors who come and dupe people that they are performing miracles.

Some time back in 2008 there came a pastor from West Africa who started a church in Kampala. It was said that he was using a battery powered gadget which they said he used to kick people and shocked them to cause a fake slain in the Spirit. Even though people wanted a bold Church leader in the Body of Christ to warn their people of such false prophets but the Pastors freaked and shied away, fearing that it would bring shame in the Born-Again Churches instead of warning their flocks. The Shepherds are failing to sound the trumpet when the sword is raised to come and destroy the people. Ezekiel 33:3.

It's a horrible thing indeed, e.g. in 1984 at the Church I was attending there was a rumour that there was a young man far away beyond Lugazi who was prophecying. At that time I was one of the few church members who had a car and two pastors of our church asked me to take them to see that young prophet.

It was Saturday early morning after the Friday Night prayer when we travelled there, what I saw and heard left me dumb founded. I looked at the boy who was around 18 years. All four members I took whom he prophesied upon got problems. All the two pastors ran and left the church since 1990s they live abroad, one young man started an occult church of Jesus Only Occult, the last lady preacher died in an occult of Kaswabule sect in Jinja.

After prophesying to them they insisted that they bring the false prophet boy to the Church so that they would attract many people to come and be church members after being prophesied upon. Pastors are after big numbers and not quality of a congregation. I advised them not to bring him knowing their intentions. They insisted and brought him to Kampala at the Church, and he was like a witch doctor, from morning till night people were coming for consultation, rich women started collecting him and taking him to their homes to go and prophesy to them. After some time he lost favour because many things he prophesied did not coming to pass. He confessed that he got tired of lying to people and returned to his home and confessed that all what he was telling people were lies because he wanted to earn a living. Imagine!!!

The Lord has said that Priests who are ruled by the False prophets, your doom is certain. Jeremiah 5:31. *24th March 2012*

CHAPTER TWENTY-EIGHT
LOOK FOR THE ANCIENT PATHS

LOOK FOR THE ANCIENT PATHS, stand by the ways and seek and ask for the Ancient Paths because time has come, people have gone very far and they are lost. It is not easy for one to go a long way and out there they tell him that you lost the way when you were on a certain junction. To find the correct way you have to go back to the place where you got lost and take the right path. It is annoying and frustrating and if you continue you will not reach your destination and you will be completely lost.

MANY PEOPLE HAVE GONE ASTRAY AND LEFT THE ANCIENT paths due to the fact that they found copies at the bottom and became crooked. Larry Bielat quoted Henry David Thoreau saying "Following the path of least resistance is what makes men and rivers crooked." Simple, some people do not want to work hard, they are lazy, they want easy things, young men women have joined churches of Born Again because they are deceived that you get rich quickly there is money coming from America. These lazy bones after maneuvering a few scriptures they run and start Churches, start telling lies here and there. Now there is

Internet go to café's to surf churches in Europe or America looking for who can support them.

In that manner that is how they are getting themselves in trouble by getting Gay Organizations who have all the money to give in order to hook them. One young man I know started browsing daily in Fort Portal town looking for big churches in Europe and USA to give him money. He had started good prayer and deliverance ministry and God was doing mighty and great things. When he came to tell me that he was being invited to go to Holland, I told him be careful and pray for God's guidance going to that country unless God Himself has sent you, not because you have to go where ever you feel you want to go. He insisted and went. When he returned, he brought pictures of those taking him to the devils Grotto and to reach some areas in the cave where he had to go on his knees, worshipping the devil directly.

After his return trouble started in his ministry, nearly every minister left him. He started sCampering looking for those who used to stand with him in the ministry everyone was distancing away from him. Now his whole ministry has fallen apart. Looking for the easy way will make you crooked and leave the ancient ways of the Lord because you do not want to work hard. The devil has easy riches but that is how it goes.

You do not know me and you do not know where I started, young men and women see those who have started three or four decades ago seeking the Lord and through their faithfulness He has blessed them. They start claiming the big houses, ministries, and vehicles they drive not knowing where they started.

One day I was doing my morning prayer walk which takes me at times 5-7 miles. This time I had started very early by 5.00am, I did a stretcher, climbed two steep hills as I landed and started to relax, I found boda boda men on a stage, as I passed them they said within my hearing; she is just joking, that's not exercise. But in true fact these men were ignorant, because they did not know where I started, the time I reached there I had come a long way which they did not see.

Therefore, to trace your ancient paths, do look at those who possess what they possess and say I also want that now because I can also pray and get it. It's not just pray, it's not that cosmetic prayers you have copied from pastors and prayer warriors on Prayer Mountains you call God; or Gad because pastor so and so calls Him GAD and you copy. Please develop your own prayer basing on your family back ground, marriage, job, etc. step by step until when you have cleared you path. The devil blocked your path all the way from your ancestors with heavy blockage, your prayer line pipes corroded, pray and you open up those pipelines, so you trace your ancient paths and see in the spirit where are all problems.

Many brethren think that when they pray for a few minutes, hours and they scream, croak and crack until then everyone stops and listens to his prayer. You can pray until your voice becomes hoarse, but your prayers are stopping somewhere, the principalities are blocking them. Daniel 12:9.

I knew one brother who prayed until the floor was covered with his saliva, he ended by starting a Jesus Only occult.

Many people have left the ancient paths due to material gains. In the book of Bro Olukoya that the devil called a World a conference in his opening address, after he had welcomed them he said "you see we cannot keep them from reading their Bibles, we can't keep them from knowing the truth, but can keep them lazy praying a miss so that in whatever they are doing they will not be effective. We can give them a lot of material riches so by trying to keep their riches together they will have less and less time to cause us trouble." *25th March 2012*

CHAPTER TWENTY-NINE
UNPURCHASABLE

MESSAGE, How the faithful city has become a harlot, she who was full of justice! Righteousness once lodged in her, but now murderers. Isaiah 1:21.

You are a City of the Lord, He has made everything appropriate in its time. He has also set eternity in their hearts, yet so that man will not find out the work which God has done from the beginning even to the end. Man does not know what God has done within his heart. Rick Joyner writes in his book "The Call" that when he met the Lord the Lord told him that if you put all the riches together from the whole world they cannot purchase the soul of man for only one second. That tells me that a man's soul is unpurchasable at whatever cost because the creator of the universe sits in it. That is why the Bible calls our body the Temple of the Holy God, 1 Corinthians 6:19-20 and He says if people go and join in fornication or adultery you defile the Temple of the Holy Spirit.

Therefore, it depends on what you do with yourself, if you are walking righteously or otherwise. In order to build the city of the Lord in your heart, man's soul is so large it can have control of places, wage war against the powers of darkness, it has unlimited movement, can travel anywhere to run errands, help deliver people, arrest situations; e.g. before I had never traveled to USA but the Lord wanted me to go and deliver a man who was having a family and a terrible evil spirit that used to come and possess him by turning him into a monster. Whenever that demon came over him, he wanted to destroy them, when he learnt that he was going to destroy them he ran to another state in the north. I saw in the Spirit the northern state where he ran to hide trying to avoid hurting his family. So, this particular night the Lord took me to the house of Dan where his family lived in the USA.

As I was standing there Dan came in when that demon was possessing him and he was in a raging state, he yelled at me that I told you never to come here, I will destroy you. The only command I gave the devil was "In the name of Jesus, I command you come out of him." The demon left without any resistance as the man and his family were standing with me in the living room. The Lord is the one who gave me the name of the man Dan and whole story concerning him.

We are working together with God, If He wants to send you to any part of the world to wage war or deliver His people you will be there without taking any means of transport. This does not mean that whether or not you have been to any place the Spirit of the Lord can lead you there, because it takes a speed of a thought to travel to any place in the world. Your soul travels faster than a speed of lightning to any destination.

Therefore, we have to tame our thoughts to line with the Word of God in order to be able to be used of God effectively. However, we have to continue building a city of our God in our hearts. This city is a Holy city, we have an Altar where worship and praise does not stop day or night, there is a tower which is a pillar of fire during the night and a white cloud during the day and the presence of the creator cannot be missed because there is love, forgiveness, peace and mercy in abundance.

There are no mosques, shrines, domes, Pentecostals, Charismatic, Catholics, Protestants, no brothels, no bars or pubs, and no lodges there. No thinking evil, no doing evil, and no seeing evil because it's a holy city. Only people who worship the Lord in Spirit and truth are there by a refreshing river flowing, here tired people, weary, depressed and oppressed people are comforted and the orphans and widows are cared for. This city is built in the hearts of men and it is a beautiful city.

Listen, O, heaven, and hear, O, earth; For the Lord speaks Son I have reared and brought you up, but they have revolted against me. *10th April 2012*

CHAPTER THIRTY
YOU ARE MY BRIDE

FROM 30TH MARCH 2012 I wanted to dye my hair, Clare bought me a Chinese dye which I found in the bottle were some unusual substances when I opened the lid. When I poured in water it gave me a brown colour. Witness inside me said do not use that dye, and I did not use it and Clare poured it out when she was cleaning.

In the Spirit I heard "Give this to me as you gave the rest." Meaning dying of my hair. I have been waiting for this, only one which has been remaining to give up was dying my hair. I found out later it was disgusting and messy, and I was tired of it too.

Afterwards I prayed that; Lord give me Peace and Joy in the spirit, and I promised the Lord that I will obey. He said "You are my Bride," I am going to do great things you will also not believe it. I went and straightened my hair and it looked wonderful. *2nd April 2012*

CHAPTER THIRTY-ONE
FRIENDSHIP AND RELATIONS

I GOT this message as I was meditating early in the morning that however one tried to keep friends and relationships without one binding factor it can never survive, whatever method one tries to keep it going or however determined, one struggles to sweeten it without the essence of God it cannot last.

Let it be a marriage of 70 years and without God binding it together it cannot be knotted together. I have noted that even in people who know and love the Lord with the absence of this element or prayer and scriptures at one time or another people let God down. Many Israel kings let God down e.g. Saul, Solomon, Asa, Josiah, Uzziah, etc. Let me put it like this; there are some people who do not know God at all, so the absence of God in their hearts or relationships leaves nothing to join or bind their friendships together, these fall apart.

Others know the Lord partially but they do not consider this element seriously and their friendship wears out, and in the end comes to a stop. Still there are those who know God fully, at first they walk with Him in their relationship, but due to the fact either they grow cold or they get used and get a familiar spirit and this results in taking God for granted and then disobedience creeps in.

Also, assuming spirits can take over, and check points disappear, even when the enemy starts passing on messages they take it for granted that it is the Lord talking. Yet, the enemy has come in as an angel of light and takes a corner where he keeps giving them false messages. By the time they release it is too late because they have gone very far. At this point they stop taking God seriously where by their friendships derail resulting in separation. *4th April 2012*

CHAPTER THIRTY-TWO
SELF INVOLVEMENT,
ANOTHER SPIRITUAL TRAP

THE SEED which fell among the thorns, bush and the thorns grew with it and chocked it, Luke 8:7. Got this msg on 15th, built on 16th.

IN PRAYER I WAS LED THAT, IN TODAY'S CHRISTIAN LIVES there are difficult situations which are keeping great faith under oppression, suppression, depression and that without Spiritual breakthrough in prayer, the Word, and in Fighting sin..

I likened this as garden with scotch grass, when they come to solve their problems, they only chop on top, yet underground there is a bed of knitted scotch grass, sin, which is knitted together choking every good plant sowed, e.g. my garden when we got a tractor My son went and plowed the scotch grass on top, he did not really till it throughly to remove all the veins underground because the plows were having a problem and could not go deep. Immediately the workers went out and sowed their maize and beans. As soon as the seeds germinated the scotch grass came from underground and entangled them and choked life out of maize and beans. We had to weed around the plants, cover them with polythene bags and spray the scotch grass killer around the plants, Christians need to cover around our spirit life with the blood of Jesus and spray against the Sin around us.

Spiritual traps, The underground network has bondages which was caused or came trailing after you from; Ancestral (Obwinsekuru), Family (ebika CLANS (enganda) and Parents (obuzarrano) All these bring Inabilities resulting from (okulemererwa), Witchcraft, idolatry, suicide, theft, night dancing, cannibalism, satanism, arguments and Fighting spirits, drunkenness, different inherited diseases; cancer, asthma, heart, madness, fits, etc.

Spiritual traps are found in Culture, e.g. funeral rights, marriage rituals like you jump and pick the kikarabo or kill a lion first. When children are born as twins and umbilical cords are buried at certain place, or women doing things so that their girls would not get pregnant and forget where they hid or did them.

Self involvement, another spiritual trap to avoid. It is like swearing in vain, cursing, gossiping, or rumor mongering, being in unforgiveness with unrepentant hearts because once saved always saved cult, business lies by hiking the price, giving false measures, or putting witchcrafts that you sell quickly. You say whom have I offended a trap of using witchcraft to catch thieves and not fighting for yourself.

Job entanglement traps, e.g. using witchcraft for favors, using witchcraft to secure place that you will not be given transfer, or using witchcraft for promotions or increases of salary.

Academic or professionalism spiritual traps, e.g. using fetishes to excel in your examination, excess ego to be above everybody else, or pride that you are above everyone else.

Superstitious beliefs, e.g. seeing palpitations on the upper eye or crying from lower eye. No woman should pass on this side or the other, and when you are going you should not meet man, woman, dog, etc. Clan totems, symbols of centipedes, snakes, animals, frogs, and or feces. Pouring a drink on the ground in Oblation etc.

Spiritual friends and marriage traps, e.g. drink each ones blood for covenants or agreements, making false promises and swearing before people nothing except death will separate us and you separate the next following week.

How Can We Over Come? When we come to know the Lord we need to go deep and remove every vein of embedded network of the scotch grass from under the ground and clear our garden by repenting of whatever you remember that involved you. Those things you know and those what you do not know because the Holy Spirit knows all things and even will make you remember or show you what took place.

Then you will come and have your a spiritual break through!!!

The next garden Emma plowed we had to wait the scotch grass to come out and spray it in order to completely destroy it from top to the veins which were embedded under the ground. Then we planted in our seeds to be free from scotch grass. In this garden we planted Irish potatoes and they yielded. 15th May 2012

CHAPTER THIRTY-THREE
IF I ASK YOU TO DO SOMETHING EXTRAORDINARY WILL YOU DO IT?

WENT TO EVANGELIZE AT KYARUSOZI-KYABASEGU, when I was ministering, I got a message from Alan that the tall dry tree had fallen on the latrine. Since 1999 this tree was there dry and I had told the Lord that that tree will be used to prepare a feast of thanksgiving to the Lord for the greatest things he has done. *27th April 2012*

I HAD A VISION, OUR LORD WAS SHOWING HIS WOUNDED hands to people around me one by one, when He reached me He passed me by and I asked Him why He did not show me. He said before you have already seen them.
29th April 2012

THE LORD ASKED ME IF I ASK YOU TO DO SOMETHING EXTRAORDINARY WILL YOU DO IT?

I said I am no longer going to be a rebel Lord, for the glory to your name I will do it. I was working in a banana plantation and I started counting things the Lord did in the Old Testament for the sake of His glory which were embarrassing to individuals.

- Abraham at 100 and Sarah at 90 gave birth to Isaac.
- He made Joseph, a slave,d prisoner a Prime Minister in a foreign land.
- He made Daniel an exiled foreigner Ruler in Byblon.
- He made Esther an exiled, orphan a Queen of Medes and Persia.
- He made Mordecai a Jew, a gatekeeper and Prime Minister instead of Haman The Agagite.
- Mary, the mother of our Lord, got pregnant while she was a virgin.
- Elizabeth the mother of John the Baptist got pregnant at an advanced age.

30th April 2012

We were in the village with Clare.

Message, Something which have taken long in your life is going to happen, get ready.

My prayer, Lord if this something is from you; may you please confirm it by sending me your trusted servant to confirm.

1st May 2012

IN MY PRAYERS WHEN PRAYING FOR SOMEONE, IT CAME TO my heart that Christians and Believers are praying wrong prayers for each other. When these prayers come and find you with a gap they crash on you, but when they come and find that you have a strong Defense Wall, it's like a skilled Cricket player, an Angel with strong gloves that no ball will pass him by, as a good Goalie standing in your goal posts no ball will enter into your net, cause he will kick the ball or after catching it will throw it so far. Therefore, that is how the angel kicks wrong prayers, wishes, desires and imaginations of evil wicked people who try to send them in our courts. Take counsel together, and it shall come to nought; speak the word, and it shall not stand: for God is with us, Isaiah 8:10

The Lord spoke to Isaiah: In as much these people have rejected the gently, slowly, smoothly flowing waters of Shiloah, the ways of the Lord are slow, gentle, smooth but sure, in order to reach our goals.

But people rejoice in Rezin, and the son of king Remaliah, they believe in human beings who bring to them rush, quick ways of getting to their goals, sometimes causing them to crash.

MESSAGE, THE LORD IS SAYING NOW THEREFORE BEHOLD the Lord is about to bring on them the strong and abundant waters of Euphrates which will raise over all its channels and boundaries and go over all its banks. Then it will sweep on into Judah, it will overflow and pass through, it will reach even to the neck, and the spread of its wings will fill the breadth of your land O Immanuel. A believing remnant will be broken, people, and be shattered, and give ear, all remote places of the earth, Isaiah 8:6-10. 2nd May 2012

JOHN SAW AN ANGEL WHO CAME FROM HEAVEN, HE WAS clothed in a cloud, had a rainbow around his head, his face was shining Like the sun, his feet were like pillars of fire and held in his hand a little book. He placed one of his feet on the sea and another one on the land, he roared like a lion and was answered by the thunders. Revelations 10.

After this, I longed to see God in His splendor because if an angel looks like that, how much is more beautiful is our creator and living God who said Heaven is my Throne and the Earth is my Foot Stool? *3rd May 2012*

SPENT THE DAY WORKING AT SCHOOL COMPOUND TILL LATE after six. *5th May 2012*

CHAPTER THIRTY-FOUR
WHY DO I LOOK LIKE A SOLDIER RIGHT NOW?

FROM: Gkabatalemwa
To: You
Daily Devotions and Messages
From: Gkabatalemwa
To: Sister Gertrude

"Fame is a vapor, popularity an accident, riches take wings, and only one thing endures that is character endures."

HORACE GREELEY

There is no more eloquent and effective defense than a life lived continuously and consistently in integrity. It possesses invincible power to silence your slanderers.

I am a freelancer who is supposed to go anywhere at God's order. (Sori, a Korean who was taken to heaven)

I asked another question to Him, "Lord, I have been taking myself as a bride, why do I look like a soldier right now?"

The Lord explained, "There is such armor hidden inside the clothes of every bride. It is not seen by people because it is covered by their beauty and modesty. You cannot be a bride without wearing such armor."

A bride is a bride and at the same time, warrior. She can die for her bridegroom, which is why she is armed with armor and Fights hard for him. A bride is mild outside and strong inside. She is happy with the success of others and enjoys it with them but never gets jealous of them or defames them. She cries and laughs with others. She works on making herself obedient in order to follow the footsteps of her bridegroom Jesus, who always puts himself below others and sets an example of serving others. I was kneeling on one knee, giving a deep bow, and expressing my gratitude to the Lord that gave me the armor.

Our Lord shared what a mission is with Sori, a Korean Sister, when she visited heaven and hell. "My concept of missionary is different from your concept of missionary. I call those who have the spirituality of bride and that of warrior and go to a land of mission missionaries. I do not recognize those who merely gave a dispatch service and went to a land of mission as missionaries. I do not say you are right just because you have done many things. I will say you are right when you have done what I wanted, however small it would be."

God uses those He has prepared for missions as missionaries and not those who prepare themselves for missions as missionaries. Those who go on a mission as a missionary quits or retires, but those who are called missionaries to a mission do not quit or retire, e.g. Bishop Orombi was a Bishop in Church of Uganda when he was on Mission as a Missionary he resigned to go and be used as Missionary on a Mission, and Pope Benedict on 11th

February 2013 announced his resignation that on 28th February he would resign as a Pope.

To be on a mission as a missionary there is work to accomplish, when it is finished or not one quits. But to be a Missionary on a Mission is a life long time commitment you serve as long as you live until you expire, e.g. Sis Agnes and Sis Judi.

Be careful not to be seduced by external phenomena and always act with love so that it will become easier to tell whether a thing is the result of love or not. Those who act with love can tell whether a thing has been done with love and figure out its true meaning.

Be careful. Those corrupted ones should not be taken lightly. They will make use of all kinds of tricks and schemes to drag you to a dark place. As a matter of fact, they are already doing it. You are so ignorant about the spiritual world and this is an act of demons that you may undergo many evil things without even knowing it.

Therefore, you should always have your spiritual eyes focused on Jesus, direct your spiritual ears towards Jesus, and work hard to praise and pray to Jesus. Do not take a break from your relationship with Jesus.

Ask Jesus to take care of your soul, stand guard for your soul during sleep, and keep the evil enemy from planting the seeds of evil in your spiritual garden using dreams and visions.

How pearls are made by oysters, irritation occurs when the shell of the oyster is invaded by an alien substance like a grain of sand. When that happens, all the resources within the tiny, sensitive oyster rush to the irritated spot and begin to release healing fluids, tears or salivas, that otherwise would have remained dormant. By and by the irritant is covered over and over again and a pearl is made from the coating fluids when they become solid.

This pearl system is not some prophetically speculative heresay or futuristic fairy tale but a real world process. It is not some whacko conspiracy theory being advanced by the fringe society. It's an orchestrated agenda which God had planned since before the foundations of the earth.

The testing of our faith is by, temptation, affliction, persecution, sickness, loneliness, difficult people, people with bad attitudes, people that treat you unfairly, anything and everything that requires patience, resolve and discipline. It's in going through these things that your faith grows. When we see others go through these things, we will see how real their faith is. Matthew 7:21-29.

I pay adoration to the author of my being!!! The divine majesty, God, does not consult when showing mercy!!! Our enemy desires to ruin our souls with malice!!! When satan is most sure of himself that he has finished me the snare is broken and I have escaped.

obu sitani amanyira kimu nti amaziire kunkwasa,
ekiriba kye aba antegere kiba
kimazire okucweka kandi nyowe maize okurabaho. *14th June 2013*

CHAPTER THIRTY-FIVE
THE JOURNEY HAS STARTED

MY HEART WAS UPLIFTED and praising the Lord a word came from the Lord: Take thee a great roll, and write in it with a man's pen ... E L AL AM ... Elalam as in Isaiah 8:1, Maher-shalal-hash-baz. In the Heavenly language one word means a thousand words and a thousand words means one word as it says that one day in the presence of the Lord means a thousand years and a thousand Years means one Day. So, I bless the Lord for His Mercies. *6th May 2012*

IN THE SPIRIT I FELT THAT THE TOORO KINGDOM ANTHEM should not be sang for the reasons that the Tooro Anthem blasphemies God. They turned the words in Psalms to suit the earthly kings, because it has words which equalize the earthly king with God, words which exalts the king against God, it does not mention God anywhere, and it brings a curse on the school.

The king is also God's subject but they involved in idolatry, satan worshipers called satanists who sacrifice humans and animals living a double standard at night they do satanist rituals and during the day they go to church. No river can bring sweet water and at the same time bring bitter water, James 3:11. *8th May 2012*

I RETURNED TO THE CITY FROM THE VILLAGE WHERE I HAD spent three weeks weeding, sowing the beans and maize, designing the compound, monitoring the school building, mending fences, etc. *10th May 2012*

I SPENT TIME WITH CLARE IN THE OFFICE PRAYING FROM 6.45pm to 8.00pm. When we were returning home the truck had a neglected problem with the clutch and another car crushed behind us and got damages. *12th May 2012*

WHILE MEDITATING I SAW A MOST BEAUTIFUL ROUND BLUE twin tower standing in a blue sky and as if it was wrapped, I saw it being unwrapped. This is the second time for me to see it. Again, I saw a square red brick altar with white smoke coming out, then another altar with burning fire. All these I saw them as if standing in the middle of Amber house. *13th May 2012*

... AS HE SAID THE JOURNEY HAS STARTED. 14TH MAY 2012

THE JOURNEY HAS STARTED   161

*Nyamabuga Foundation Schools in 2018.
Our school has more than 400 students*

LEARN MORE AT WWW.NEEPUGANDA.ORG

ACKNOWLEDGMENTS

SCHULLER, ROBERT, *Tough Times Never Last, But Tough People Do*, Bantam; Reissue edition 1984

RICK JOYNER, *The Call*, Morningstar Publications, 2006

TOMMY TENNY, *The God Chasers: My Soul Follows Hard After Thee*, Destiny Image Publishers; 16th edition 1998

JOHN MASON, *You're Born an Original--Don't Die a Copy*, Revell; Reprint edition 2011

ABOUT THE AUTHOR

The late Gertrude Kabatalemwa labored for the kingdom of God in her native land of Uganda. The burden of her heart was for the good news of Jesus to become deeply rooted, firmly grounded, and abundantly fruitful in the lives of the people of Uganda. In the past, she has served her nation as secretary to the president. She also functioned as Minister for the Development of Women.

At one point, she had taken in thirty-five of the orphans into her own village home, subsequently establishing Nyamabuga Foundational Schools for village children. Her plans include to prepare and equip these young people with the skills necessary to be able to lead their nation with a moral worldview.

Today, her children and those that she has poured into continue her work.

Through this book, you will be blessed by encountering the very large heart of this precious servant of God.

This is Gertrude's third book of the series "My Deepest Heart's Devotions."

facebook.com/Neepuganda

www.ingramcontent.com/pod-product-compliance
Lightning Source LLC
Chambersburg PA
CBHW052133110526
44591CB00012B/1708